SHIKOKU

Wisdom for the Wayfarer

by **YVONNE CORPUZ**

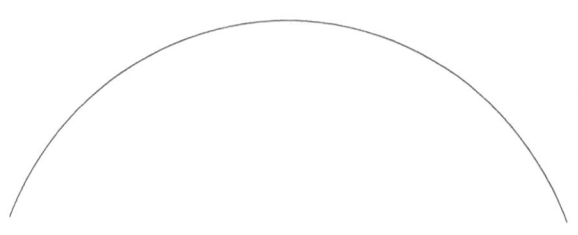

For Roberto, Paolo and John and their families,
who travelled many roads with me
in our journeys together,

and in loving memory of my parents,
Renato and Gundena Asprer,
who first lit my path.

To those who come after us,
may these words light yours.

CONTENTS

THE PAUSE — **7**

PART I

THE NUDGE — **13**
STORIES AND SURPRISES — 15
Koyasan

PART II

THE JOURNEY — **25**
THE DAY BEFORE: QUESTIONS AND QUESTS — 27
Haneda Airport, Tokyo

DAY 1: ROUTES AND RITUALS — 35
Temples 1 to 17: Tokushima Prefecture

DAY 2: LEGENDS AND LANDSCAPES — 71
Temples 18 to 23: Tokushima Prefecture

DAY 3: MYTHS AND MOUNTAINS — 97
Temples 24 to 34: Kochi Prefecture

DAY 4: SIGHTS AND SOUNDS — 121
Temples 35 to 39: Kochi Prefecture

DAY 5: PRESENCE AND PURPOSE — 143
Temples 40 to 51: Ehime Prefecture

DAY 6: FAITH AND FREEDOM — 167
Temples 52 to 64: Ehime Prefecture

DAY 7: RENDEZVOUS AND REDEMPTION — 185
Temple 65: Ehime Prefecture
Temples 66 to 79: Kagawa Prefecture

DAY 8: COMPLETION AND CELEBRATION — 207
Temples 80 to 88: Kagawa Prefecture

PART III

THE RETURN HOME	**223**
MONKS AND MYSTERIES	225
Koyasan	
PROMISE AND POSSIBILITY	249
Sydney, Australia	

PART IV

OUR ITINERARY:	
BY CAR TO 88 TEMPLES IN 8 DAYS	**257**
DAY 1: TOKUSHIMA PREFECTURE	260
(DOJO OF SPIRITUAL AWAKENING):	
Temples 1 to 17	
DAY 2: TOKUSHIMA PREFECTURE	261
(DOJO OF SPIRITUAL AWAKENING):	
Temples 18 to 23	
DAY 3: KOCHI PREFECTURE	262
(DOJO OF ASCETIC TRAINING):	
Temples 24 to 34	
DAY 4: KOCHI PREFECTURE	263
(DOJO OF ASCETIC TRAINING):	
Temples 35 to 39	
DAY 5: EHIME PREFECTURE	264
(DOJO OF ENLIGHTENMENT):	
Temples 40 to 51	
DAY 6: EHIME PREFECTURE	265
(DOJO OF ENLIGHTENMENT):	
Temples 52 to 64	
DAY 7: EHIME PREFECTURE	266
(DOJO OF ENLIGHTENMENT):	
Temple 65	

KAGAWA PREFECTURE (DOJO OF NIRVANA): Temples 66 to 79	266
DAY 8 : KAGAWA PREFECTURE (DOJO OF NIRVANA): Temples 80 to 88	267

PART V

NOTES	269
ENDNOTES	270
SELECTED REFERENCES	274
GLOSSARY	276
IN GRATITUDE	278
ABOUT THE AUTHOR	279

THE PAUSE

ALL HEALING, IT IS said, takes place in the pause between the exhale and the inhale. The exhale creates the space for the next abundant inhale.

With the Covid pandemic, I felt like I was in some pause. It was as though the virus had put aspects of my life on hold and left me uncertain about how to proceed. I wondered whether others shared a similar experience. Untethered to familiar routines, conversations with family and friends revolved around making different, better choices in a quest to live life more fully. This pause in time deepened my desire to live in a more conscious, engaged and harmonious way with the universe surrounding me and the universe of thoughts and feelings within me.

My musings led to two realisations. First, while international travel remained heavily restricted, I could still relish the memories of past journeys and savour these with gratitude and greater appreciation. Second, I could develop new skills as an avenue for creative expression and meaningful pursuit. The unexpected gift of time that the pandemic presented was the perfect opportunity to act on my ideas. Thus, this book took shape – *Shikoku: Wisdom for the Wayfarer*.

For most of my 40-year career, I was in senior strategic HR leadership roles in top global organisations. My most vital contributions were in talent management and learning, capability building and culture transformation. I believe my gifts were empowering leaders to enhance their teams' performance, inspiring people to embrace their magnificence and being an impactful role model for emerging women leaders in a largely male-dominated environment. I was passionate about my work, enjoyed it tremendously and excelled at it. I held regional and global roles in the

Philippines, Hong Kong, Australia, Singapore and Japan. To love what you do and to know that it all makes a positive difference – how blessed I was. It was my service to humanity, my 'love made visible', paraphrasing the Lebanese poet Kahlil Gibran.

But life has its twists and turns. In 2018, my expatriate assignment in Tokyo was unexpectedly curtailed. Just shy of 18 months in Japan, I was to be repatriated to my home city of Sydney, Australia, to take on another global role. I was personally devastated and professionally disillusioned. I had fallen in love with Japan and was convinced that my global perspective added tremendous value and my inclusive style of leadership was helping to shape the company in transformational ways. A well-respected colleague talked of the work we had accomplished together as 'jewels in the crown' of the company. Suddenly, I felt like a bird whose wings had been clipped in mid-flight. A sense of disappointment overwhelmed me. I could not shake off the despondency and uncertainty that haunted me.

Ironically, over the past many years, I had facilitated countless Change Management workshops, coached leaders one-on-one to manage personal and professional transitions and mentored them to overcome obstacles and achieve their goals. Yet here I was, seemingly unable to rise above the deeply distressing circumstances and purposefully embrace a new direction in my life.

I felt I had to get away for a while, distract myself from the inconvenient truths of derailed personal plans, and find some diversion somewhere. But where?

During my first months in Tokyo, a Japanese friend had piqued my interest in the Shikoku pilgrimage. He spoke excitedly about this 1,400-kilometre circuit (some say 1,200, depending on how one navigates and travels) around the perimeter of Shikoku, the smallest and most obscure of Japan's four main islands. Eighty-eight official temples dot the island. Every temple has some historical tradition or legend, some statue or image associated with or ascribed to the Buddhist saint Kukai, referred to posthumously as Kobo Daishi. This, even if there is little evidence to show that the historical Kobo Daishi actually visited these sites.[1]

I was to discover later that Kobo Daishi (774–835 C.E.), one of the most revered Buddhist monks, was the recognised founder of the Shingon sect of Buddhism in Japan. He was an accomplished man who impacted the evolution of Japanese culture and history with his tremendous contributions.[2]

I knew that Japan had hundreds of pilgrimage routes. But I had not realised that this was one of the most celebrated journeys in a country well known for its pilgrimage culture.[3] My friend told me that this Shikoku *henro* (Shikoku pilgrimage) or Shikoku *hachijuhachi kasho* (88 sacred sites of Shikoku) was the best known among the Japanese.

The undertaking is often compared to the world-famous Camino de Santiago. Also known as the Way of St James, this Catholic pilgrimage consists of a network of routes across Europe that ends in the city surrounding the Cathedral of Santiago de Compostela in Spain. Shikoku *henro* in Japan is different, however, because it is a circular pilgrimage, and one can begin or end at any place in that loop.

My friend aroused my curiosity further when he assured me that I would be awed by the natural beauty of this remote island, have the rare opportunity to glimpse 'deep Japan' and be forever touched by the kindheartedness and generosity of the locals. I was immediately captivated by the prospect of completing this 88-temple pilgrimage. But there never seemed to be an opportune time to do it.

In mid-2019, five months after I had relocated from Tokyo to Sydney, it seemed to be the perfect moment for this diversion, this distraction. So, I packed my bags and decided to travel to the 88 main temples of Shikoku. While there are many options of how to make the pilgrimage, as you will learn, my journey to the 88 temples was by car, making possible its completion in eight days.

Although I was not seeking any epiphany about life, this journey turned out to be my 'healing pause between the exhale and the inhale'. Instead of a diversion from self, the adventure helped me reconnect to my authentic self with kindness and compassion. Instead of being a distraction, the experiences on the pilgrimage enabled me to rediscover a shift from focusing on obstacles to seeing joyful possibilities. Indeed, Shikoku reawakened a wisdom of the heart that rekindled a sense of inner peace in me.

Come, be my travel companion. Share this journey with me now in *Shikoku: Wisdom for the Wayfarer*.

Yvonne Corpuz
Sydney, Australia
January 2024

I

THE NUDGE

Stories

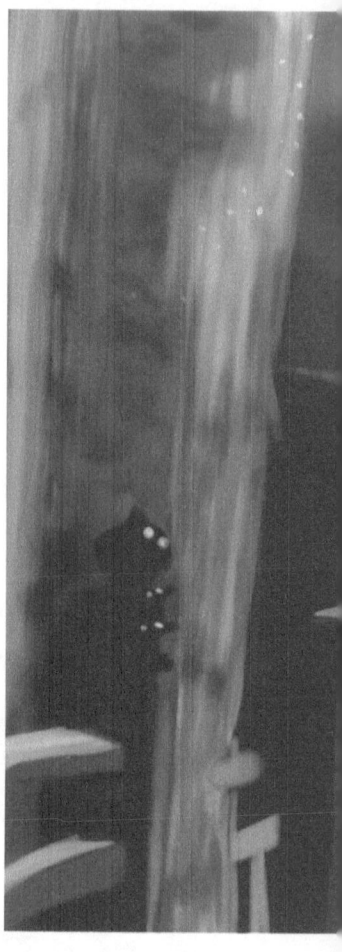

and

Surprises

THIS IS THE STARTING point for the Shikoku pilgrimage – Mount Koya in Wakayama Prefecture in south-eastern Japan. I did not know this when I stood atop the beautiful, mysterious Koyasan, as it is affectionately called, on a dark night in October 2017. Koyasan, though customarily translated as Mount Koya, is not a mountain but a basin-like plateau – the '*san*' in this case indicates a sacred place. Although the night was dark, it was not moonless. I recall a monk asking, 'What is the shape of the mind?' In the darkness, I stood, formulating my response.

This is also the ending point for the pilgrimage – Mount Koya in Wakayama Prefecture in south-eastern Japan. Although Koyasan is not located in Shikoku, nor is it one of the 88 temples, the tradition is that one comes back to report to the Buddhist priest Kobo Daishi that the pilgrimage has been completed. I did not know that then either. Nor did I know that I would be back two years later to do precisely that.

I only knew then that the priest Kukai – later honoured by the title 'Kobo Daishi', meaning 'the great teacher who spread the Buddhist teachings widely' – had passed from this life but was not considered dead by his followers. Instead, they believed he was in a state of eternal meditation in a mausoleum in Okunoin, a vast graveyard on this very mountain. Whether or not one recognises this as so, it remains a central belief of many Buddhists, especially those of the Shingon sect. And I only knew that from the stories I heard that weekend.

It was a day in March 835 C.E., so the story goes. The revered monk had been ill for some time and had predicted the day of his passing.[1] His disciples waited

> The mind is shaped like the moon –
> Sometimes it is closed.
> Sometimes it is open.
> Or somewhere in between.
> And while the moon has no light of its own,
> it reflects the wondrous light from the One Mind.

anxiously. Throngs of villagers began their trek to Mount Koya and kept vigil in the courtyard.

His disciples saw that his eyes were closed, but he sat upright as though in deep meditation. He remained in the same position for seven days, then another seven days, and yet another seven days. The faithful disciples held a memorial service and then another. But his body was left undisturbed as he appeared to be in deep meditation.

Details are ambiguous, but the story goes on to say that on the forty-ninth day, Kobo Daishi's disciples reported a few noteworthy developments. His body was warm and moist to the touch. His hair and beard had grown, and he needed a shave.

Accounts are again unclear. What prevails is the story that Kobo Daishi transcended death. So, in this mausoleum in Okunoin, a lamp is kept burning, and food is brought in twice a day.

This mausoleum is the focal point of the cemetery and the most venerated site in all of sacred Koyasan. For this reason alone, Okunoin is the heart of Koyasan and Koyasan is the heart of spirituality in the Japanese archipelago.

The sanctuary of Koyasan lies some 322 kilometres southwest of Mount Fuji. It consists of a flatland in a valley elevated at a modest altitude of 800 metres. Eight 1,000-metre-high mountain peaks surround it. In the lyrical language of poetry, Koyasan has been described as a lotus flower with eight petals.

Kobo Daishi introduced Shingon to Japan, the school of Buddhism that teaches the secret path to attain enlightenment within one's lifetime. He established its headquarters on Mount Koya over 1,200 years ago when it was no more than a remote mountain wilderness. His followers gradually built meditation huts, then temples, lecture halls and other buildings. The construction continued even after Kobo Daishi had entered his final rest. Today, this monastic centre has evolved into a sprawling complex of over a hundred monasteries and temples. Many of these serve as inns that host hundreds of pilgrims and visitors annually. It is now listed as a UNESCO World Heritage Site.[2]

In this tranquil valley is a small town with shops and restaurants that cater to all who are drawn to this peaceful haven. The devoted pilgrims and the curious travellers. The zealous priests of Shingon Buddhism and its diligent students. Even the schoolchildren on summer outings. Across its many temples are heard rhythmic chanting, the beat of a drum, the chiming of a bell or a distant gong, punctuated by the occasional muted honking of a passing car. This is all a part of the significant legacy of Kobo Daishi, who changed the religious landscape of Japan.

This man was known to be a poet, writer, sculptor, painter, calligrapher, civil engineer, architect and educator. He was a noteworthy contributor to the development of the Japanese kana script that helped ordinary people read without having to learn thousands of Chinese characters. Because of him, people wanted their own graves to be in Okunoin, close to the resting place of Kobo Daishi. Indeed, today it is the site of the memorials or graves of many prominent and notable persons in Japanese history.

The birthplace of this much-beloved monk was Shikoku. Simply because of this fact, the pilgrimage to Shikoku has endured for over a thousand years. The reverence surrounding this 'great teacher' extended to the trails he is said to have walked and the sites he is said to have visited.

I knew nothing of the Shikoku pilgrimage then, nor was I even remotely interested. But seeds with the potential of birthing new possibilities are planted – who knows how or why – in the most unexpected moments.

I am standing in an aisle of a huge gift shop in Koyasan when an elegant album-like book of creamy double-folded paper catches my eye. I have always loved beautiful stationery – journals, notebooks and writing paper. For a brief moment, I fumble in lifting the cover because the book is meant to be opened from the back, as is the Japanese way. I slowly flip through the pages displaying finely detailed artistic sketches of edifices. There are elevated wooden structures, simple yet dignified, and curvy, elongated roofs, graceful yet solid. Doorways open to reveal flights of steps, or stone lanterns or elegant walkways framed with wispy trees. Japanese characters dance in the space below the drawings in delicate, brushed calligraphy. In between each of the illustrated pages is a blank page.

Though I have no idea what it is to be used for, I feel compelled to buy this book. I do not know then that it is to become a compass for a significant new adventure. When I take it in my hands, its pages then empty, I have not the slightest inkling that I will embark one day on the fascinating adventure to the 88 sacred sites on the remote island of Shikoku.

A month after my Koyasan weekend, I meet up in Tokyo with my good friend Shin. And that is where the mystery unravels.

'Let's celebrate,' declares Shin, his mug of San Miguel beer raised high in the air.

I motion a jubilant '*Kanpai!* Cheers.'

Shin and I first connected some years earlier in a training workshop in the Philippines, the land of my birth. He introduced me to this excellent Filipino restaurant in Roppongi when I relocated from Singapore to Tokyo, a career move that marked yet another pioneering global role. It soon became one of our favourite haunts, and we shared many a meal here. On one occasion, it was the completion of his doctorate studies. On another occasion he joined me as I hosted a first-ever Filipino dinner-cum-karaoke for Japanese colleagues from my workplace in Marunouchi, the financial district of Tokyo.

Today, we are celebrating my return from the mysterious Koyasan.

I take great care when unwrapping my book with its intricately designed brocade cover of interwoven blue, gold and white threads. Then I show Shin this treasure that I bought in Koyasan.

'Oh, that's a beautiful *nokyocho*, a pilgrim's stamp book,' he exclaims.

Puzzled, I ask earnestly, 'What is it used for?'

Shin excitedly explains that this pilgrim's stamp book is used for the 88-temple pilgrimage in Shikoku. Every other page has a sketch of each of its 88 temples. The temple's name, its central object of reverence and a poem appear in beautiful Japanese calligraphy at the bottom of the drawings.

He elaborates that the pages of the *nokyocho* are intended to be stamped with vermilion seals that represent the primary image enshrined in the temple's main hall. The temple steward then handwrites the temple's name in kanji (the Chinese characters used in the Japanese writing system), using black ink over the red imprints. A powerful array of calligraphic brushstrokes artfully indicates the name of the hall and, in some temples, the date of the visit.

In both ancient tradition and present-day times, these vermilion seals are valuable as evidence that one has indeed visited those temples or shrines.[3] Shin tells me stories of how these completed pilgrim's stamp books are seen as the equivalent of a passport to the heavenly realm as they represent the karmic merit accumulated through visits to sacred places. Indeed, on a later visit to one of the temples, I meet a Japanese man, Nobu-san, who tells me he placed all of his seven fully stamped pilgrim's books in his mother's coffin to accompany her to the afterlife. Hence he was again collecting stamps in preparation for the end of his own earthly journey.

At precisely that moment, Sayuri, the restaurant manager, interrupts with a plate of sizzling *sisig*. This well-seasoned, fried chopped pork is a Filipino dish that Anthony Bourdain, the late American celebrity chef and travel documentarian, once said would 'win the hearts and minds of the world'.

'*Arigato gozaimasu.* Thank you very much,' I say and signal a thumbs-up to Tara, her husband, the restaurant's chef. The warm experience of *omotenashi*, the unparalleled Japanese concept of exceptional and wholehearted service, always transforms our simple meal into an elaborate feast.

Shin and I talk in between mouthfuls of the *sisig* and a delicious spicy stew of pork cubes, chillies, coconut milk and shrimp paste, accompanied by a nice cold mug of San Miguel beer. I listen to his descriptions of the pilgrimage.

I find myself enraptured by this distant island in the south of Japan. He tells me how much he admires Kobo Daishi and how proud he is that his family belongs to the Shingon sect, one of the leading schools of Buddhism in Japan. Shin calls him 'St Kobo Daishi' – primarily for my benefit, I think, as he knows I am a Catholic. I smile briefly and glance embarrassedly at the floor. In truth, I am a lukewarm Catholic who finds every reason possible to miss Sunday Mass.

As he speaks about Shikoku, I feel that silent nudge, a prompt I sometimes get when I am being led to action by some inner wisdom. And this, well, this is that nudge – perfect for the restless and curious traveller I am, seeking to explore and be awed by the natural beauty, culture and history of this unique country. I smile as I dare to imagine the possibilities, knowing it is so.

The waning autumn moonlight filters through the half-open door of the restaurant. I glance at Sayuri as she puts away some chairs and cleans the counter. I sense that we have stayed past their usual closing time, though she is much too gracious to send us packing. I wrap the book carefully and return it to my bag as we leave, even more intrigued by it.

I did not know then that I would become a *henro* (or *ohenro*, the '*o*' being used as a polite prefix), as the pilgrims to these 88 temples are called. Nor was I aware that many pilgrims start and end their journey at Koyasan. In hindsight, having just been to Koyasan, I had serendipitously somehow already begun the journey.

What I did know was that the stage had been set. Shikoku was beckoning me, but it would be two more years before I heeded the call.

> Perhaps,
> intention creates the space
> for magnificent
> opportunities
> to emerge.
> And the journey starts
> even before the trip begins.

II

THE JOURNEY

THE DAY BEFORE

Questions

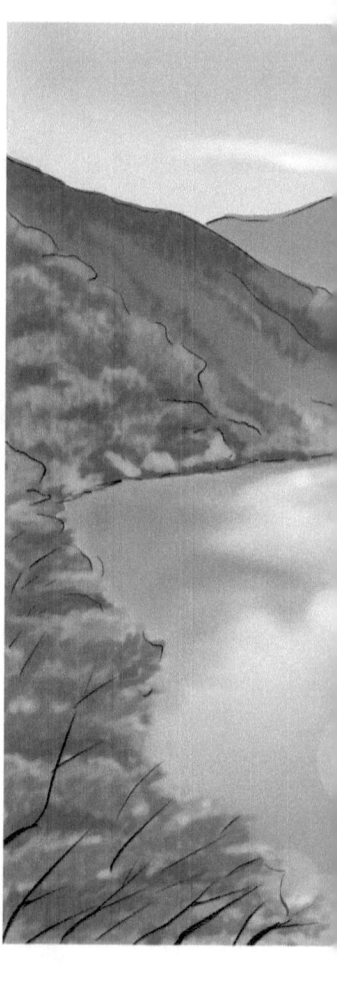

and

Quests

TOKYO

Haneda Airport

MANY THINGS CAN HAPPEN in two years. And many things did.

During that time, I developed a deep love for Japan. Living on my own in Tokyo, with family far away in Australia, I discovered the enjoyable hobby of exploring temples and shrines. It was a lens through which I could deeply appreciate Japanese culture, history, geography and tradition.

Anyone who has been to Japan will likely have noticed the ubiquitous presence of convenience stores. It may be a surprise, however, to learn that temples and shrines are even more commonplace. Available information suggests that there are almost three times more temples and shrines than convenience stores across the country.

Putting intention to attention, I realised that my journeying was not about religion but reverence. It was not so much about paying homage to a deity as honouring a people, their stories, their land. Allowing myself to be surprised, I found it was recreation and renewal. The world is as bountiful, as remarkable and as capable of touching the depths of our souls as we are willing to let it.

I immersed myself in these experiences not to 'get away from things' but precisely because I wanted to 'get deeper into things'. Beyond the veil of luminous awareness, I would sense a touch of mystery, the stirring of the Divine. I began to be mindful of what I was noticing – whether I was climbing steep stone steps, breathing in the sublime radiance of an orange sky at sundown, or standing still on a spot with the brooding presence of a thousand years of mystery.

But in the shifting sands of time, there came a bittersweet moment for me. Quite unexpectedly, as I mentioned, I was repatriated to Sydney, which is home to me. I had mixed emotions as I was not completely aligned with the reasons for my move. I felt I had unfinished business in Japan, and leaving the country at that time, even for a new Sydney-based role in my company, crushed my spirit. I was weighed down by some resentment from the whole experience. Having spent many years away from Australia because of my expatriate career, part of me looked forward to being back with family in Sydney. But I let the negativity colour aspects of my transition, so my return to Australia was not as joyful an experience as it could have been.

I have discovered the reality that change, even positive, brings a sense of loss. And transitions have a way of amplifying apprehensions and fears.

But this is a new chapter. Today is the twenty-eighth of April 2019, and I am on my way to Tokyo, not for work but to pursue a dream – the Shikoku pilgrimage. And this time, the trip is for me to 'get away from things'.

I look out of the window excitedly as the plane lands at Haneda International Airport in Tokyo. I have made this trip from Australia countless times. But now, new anticipation enlivens my heart.

Tomorrow, I will be journeying to Shikoku with Mayumi and Katsuji. Mayumi is a dear friend and a knowledgeable tour guide who has accompanied me on many adventures around Japan. Katsuji is her husband, whom I will be meeting for the first time.

I recall a conversation with Mayumi just before I departed from Tokyo five months ago. We conversed warmly over a meal of delicious *soba*, Japanese noodles made from buckwheat flour, and *tempura*, which is prawns or vegetables fried in a light batter.

'Mayumi,' I said, 'you know how much I have always enjoyed our trips together. There must be something special about the Shikoku pilgrimage – I can't get it out of my head. It feels like this is one adventure we need to go on.' I said this with deep emotion, and my voice sounded somewhat strange, even to me.

'Ah,' Mayumi replied in her usual upbeat manner, 'I've often heard how special the Shikoku *henro* is. I have never been to Shikoku, so I would be excited to go on this adventure with you.'

'*Yoroshiku onegaishimasu*,' I said, using that quintessential Japanese phrase that conveys in the same breath 'please help me' and 'thank you in advance for how you will be doing your best to help me'. This is a complex, highly nuanced 'situational' phrase with no direct English translation. But it is so deeply ingrained in Japanese culture that Mayumi understands that I am entrusting to her care not only my request but also myself in this journey.

And now I am here in Tokyo because we have a travel plan for Shikoku. Having decided that we would make the pilgrimage by car, Mayumi and Katsuji painstakingly researched the itinerary. They determined the details of our driving route and overnight accommodation and coordinated our travel schedules.

My pace quickens as I head to the airport hotel with its crisp, clean sheets and pillows filled with the hard outer casings of buckwheat seeds so that they mould closely to the head and neck. What a reassuring welcome for a brief respite of one night. Ah, the ease and comfort of the simple and uncomplicated.

As my eyes scan the street scene, I imagine myself again in downtown Tokyo – one of my favourite cities in the world. A city of cities, it is at once modern, mysterious, refined, elusive and enigmatic. The old and the new, the past and the present coalesce, constant yet ever-changing.

If there ever were a place that I could call my second home, this would be it. Here, where new adventures and fresh memories are forever being created. Here, where countless stories are shared.

Though undeniably tired from the long flight and the tedious work of the preceding days, I am too excited to sleep. So I cast my eyes again over the itinerary Mayumi sent me some days ago. I had no additional input to offer and was happy to agree to the plan she and Katsuji had drawn up.

Suddenly, a slight unease grips me. Do I have everything I need for this trip?

I look at the hard-shell carry-on bag that lies half-open on my bed. I have crammed into it my clothes and footwear for the next eight days. In my backpack are my precious *nokyocho*, a large Japanese map of Shikoku detailing each temple's location, and the 2018 paperback edition of *Shikoku Japan 88 Route Guide* by Tateki Miyazaki and Naoyuki Matsushita. This compact guidebook is the only book I have with me on this trip. It contains valuable and practical information on many aspects of the pilgrimage.

On page one of the route guide, I find the following reassuring words:

> What is most important is not reaching the goal, but the journey itself. The warm hearts of the people you meet and the beautiful nature of Shikoku you see will perfectly complement your action of doing the pilgrimage.

Yes, it is the journey that is the most important. To make it a truly immersive experience, I decided to bring only the barest of life's essentials. Travel light, I told myself. Travel light.

Unlike on other trips, I have brought no other book or reading materials. Besides my iPhone, I have unyoked myself from any devices and gadgets. Still, I am uneasy about having left my laptop in Sydney – some 8,000 kilometres away. I am already feeling unsettled that I do not have this most indispensable of tools with me. How will I survive our eight-day trip without this?

I call my husband in Sydney to tell him that I have arrived safely in Tokyo and how eagerly I am looking forward to my trip to Shikoku. 'I'm just looking at the things I packed,' I tell him. 'I decided not to bring my laptop and am suddenly wondering if I have everything I need for my trip.'

Roberto hears the slight panic in my voice. He reassures me, saying, 'Yes, you already have everything you need for this trip. You bring an open mind. You have an attentive and receptive heart. You are sensitive to the promptings of the Spirit. Yes, you already have everything you need for this trip.'

My spirit is soothed. My worries fall away. I find my inner calm again. Roberto is my steadfast anchor in life. How supportive he has always been of me. He has encouraged me to pursue my dreams and follow my heart all these many years. I say to myself, I hope he knows I am always here for him too. And then I send a kiss his way on the wings of a prayer.

I wanted to speak with our two sons too. But Paolo and John have lives of their own now. One is out with friends, watching a football game in a stadium. The other is out to dinner with his wife. They were just young boys when I first had the opportunity to travel internationally for work. I would return home from my trips with exciting toys for them. As the frequency of my travels increased significantly, the only thing they asked me to bring back were stories of places and things I had seen or experienced.

We would be together on road trips or sitting around the dinner table or in relaxed conversation before they went to bed. I would tell them about the first-ever Broadway production of *Les Misérables* I watched in New York with my sisters-in-law. Or the match between two popular Premier League teams that I caught on a television in a London pub while nursing an ankle sprain. Or the Olympic Museum in Lausanne in Switzerland that I visited during an executive course with a business school in the area.

And even now that they are young men, I still regale them with stories of my travels over coffee or a nice hot meal at home. What stories will I bring them this time, I wonder, from my Shikoku adventure?

It is towards midnight when sleep overtakes me. It seems as though I am gliding effortlessly through a verdant meadow. I enjoy a rest peaceful enough to make me feel fully relaxed, but light enough to stir me even before my alarm clock alerts me for our early-morning flight to Shikoku.

> The familiar fades,
> edged out by the strange, the new,
> in a journey of joyful expectation.
> Divine adventure beckons;
> let wonder unfold.

DAY 1

Routes

and

Rituals

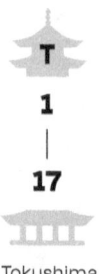

Tokushima Prefecture

THE AIRPORT IS PACKED. It is the weekend before Japan's Golden Week, which consists of four national holidays, all within seven days. We are making the pilgrimage at this time precisely for this reason. However, some guidebooks caution against this, as the week is a popular Japanese holiday season, and it will be busy on the roads. But going precisely now will make spending time away from home and work manageable.

Eagerly awaiting our turn for boarding, Mayumi and I talk excitedly. I meet Katsuji for the first time, and his cheerful manner and sense of fun put me at ease. He practises his rudimentary English with me, and I practise my basic Japanese with him. Mayumi laughs when I say that Katsuji is doing better with his English than I am with my Japanese.

We plant ourselves in our seats on the plane and settle into the 90-minute flight. Katsuji is reviewing the papers for our car rental arrangement. Taking advantage of the Golden Week holidays and with practical considerations of time and physical fitness, we intend to drive to all 88 temples in eight days.

The number eight jumps out at us, and we agree that this seems serendipitous. In many cultures, eight is considered an auspicious number, its shape associated with perfection and infinity. The kanji character for *hachi* – number eight – comprises two slightly curved descending lines.

The distance between these lines is narrow at the top but then broadens with the downward stroke, implying growth or an increase in prosperity. Yet the number eight is not only about power and strength but also balance and harmony. These are all qualities that will serve us well in our pilgrimage.

I surreptitiously glance around the plane, wondering if any passengers plan to walk this route of over a thousand kilometres. That would likely take 50 or 60 days, not to mention the physical strain of walking 20 to 30 kilometres a day on all kinds of terrain. I try to imagine how they would navigate the ancient forest trails, scenic paths through the countryside and strenuous tracks up rugged mountain slopes, past the sweet-smelling fruit groves and into the alluring fragrance of cedars. I picture them drumming their steps on unforgiving concrete roads and harsh asphalt on long, wearying stretches between temples. Or perhaps someone is planning to circumnavigate the island by bike? That would take about 20 days, while going by train or bus would take around 10 days.

I heave a sigh, relieved that there is no single prescribed way to complete the pilgrimage. I feel that this flexibility must entice a great many people into making the journey. In an open invitation to all, the pilgrimage draws into its embrace pilgrims of all faiths and nationalities. It matters not one's purpose or intention, drive or motivation. All that is expected is a receptive heart, a respectful attitude and a considerate disposition.

I look across the aisle again at Katsuji as he traces a route on a road map with his finger. I try to catch any subtle signs of concern or hesitancy.

Months ago, Mayumi told me that some of Shikoku's roads are so narrow that only a small car can drive them. Yet these same roads are two-way. I recall our phone conversation one night when she told me that there are blind bends, confusing junctions and no guardrails on terrifyingly steep and narrow mountain passes. We were then uncertain who would be adept enough to drive for those eight days in such unfamiliar territory.

Isn't that a great metaphor for life? No matter how one decides to make their pilgrimage, a *henro* must constantly navigate the challenges and the obstacles encountered, I thought to myself at that time.

However, in a completely unexpected turn of events, an excellent solution emerged that had seemed an improbable option at the beginning of our planning. Katsuji, a very experienced driver, expressed his interest in journeying with us, motivated by the prospect of making some YouTube videos about it.[1] By some synchronicity, our planned trip slotted in exceptionally well with his schedules and work timetables.

As I recollect this, Katsuji turns in my direction, smiles broadly and gives me a thumbs-up.

Mayumi is perceptive, and she sees the exchange. She smiles reassuringly, and with a hand on my arm, she says, 'Don't worry. We have figured out the best routes to get from temple to temple. And Katsuji is a great driver. We will have an amazing pilgrimage together.'

I am glad we are making this journey together. In my early months in Tokyo, it was Mayumi who fuelled my interest in visiting Buddhist temples and Shinto shrines. I first met her on a humid summer's day when she introduced me to the Tokyo *jissha*, a circuit that consists of ten shrines in the Tokyo metropolitan area.[2] These are among the most beautiful and historically significant shrines in Tokyo.

After that, we explored temples all over the country, from the vibrant forests of rustic Akita, Aomori and Iwate in the northern part of Japan to hidden shrines in Okinawa, the southernmost prefecture. We went to stunning locations like Miyajima, Matsushima and Amanohashidate, designated the three most scenic spots in Japan, an enduring list attributed to Shunsai Hayashi, a Japanese neo-Confucian philosopher-writer in the seventeenth century.

With the humming of the plane's engine, I drift into my thoughts, recalling how I'd assumed that the primary attraction of these explorations was that they served my inquisitive mind. I could learn new things, gain insights into history, understand cultural expressions and perhaps even develop a level of mastery in some intriguing subject of study.

Soon, however, I came to realise that my journeys had to do with nurturing my heart. It is the heart that responds to beauty, inspiration and inner guidance. In traversing various paths to Japan's temples and shrines, I experienced a communion with nature that stirred my heart in consecration and celebration. The heart seeks a connection to the sacred, the most abiding answer to its deepest longings.

In a dreamy state, I glance out of the plane window and cast my eyes on the island we are approaching. This is Shikoku in the south-western part of Japan, south of the main island of Honshu. At 18,800 square kilometres, it is the smallest and least populated of the archipelago's four main islands. I've read that the name Shikoku means 'Four Countries', and the island indeed consists of four prefectures: Tokushima, Kochi, Ehime and Kagawa. These were previously known as the feudal domains of Awa, Tosa, Iyo and Sanuki, respectively.

I conjure up the few interesting facts I've learned about Shikoku from my colleagues. Tokushima Prefecture is the popular starting point for the Shikoku pilgrimage. It is also well known for the Awaodori Matsuri, the most famous of many dance festivals held across Japan in mid-August for the Obon season, when the spirits of one's ancestors are honoured as part of a Japanese Buddhist custom. Kochi Prefecture is home to Japan's best-preserved feudal castle of the same name. It also boasts remarkable mountain vistas and delicious fresh food from the Seto Inland Sea, sometimes referred to as Japan's Mediterranean Sea. Ehime Prefecture's Dogo Onsen is one of the oldest hot springs in Japan, acclaimed for its impressive wooden public bath house. It has become even more famous for having inspired the popular Studio Ghibli anime film *Spirited Away*. And Japan's most recognisable noodle dish, *sanuki udon*, hails from Kagawa Prefecture, formerly known as Sanuki.

The time on the flight goes quickly. A sense of expectancy seems to hang in the air as we land at Tokushima Awaodori Airport in Shikoku. I look at Mayumi and Katsuji, whose beaming smiles say they feel this joyful anticipation too.

I am standing by the aeroplane door as it opens to allow passengers to disembark. I feel the warm breath of the wind caress my face. A gladness animates my heart.

> It is as though
> the Universe has conspired
> to pull together
> the perfect ingredients
> for a
> Divine adventure.

Mayumi, Katsuji and I have left behind the inertia of habitual routines in familiar territories. We have crossed a new and exciting threshold. With our rented car, route guide and purposefulness in our step, our goal is clear – to visit all 88 temples in eight days.

Our journey will take us through the four prefectures of Shikoku. It is customary to divide the long list of 88 temples into four sections, each one corresponding to the geographical boundaries of the island. In turn, these four sections correspond to a stage in the sacred journey that is the pilgrimage.[3]

'We will start our journey at Naruto Town in Tokushima Prefecture, which is called the Dojo of Spiritual Awakening,' I hear Mayumi saying as she reads from her notes. 'In this context, "*dojo*" means "the place or the way to learn". Here, pilgrims hope to find the faith fundamental to spiritual progress. Then we will proceed to Kochi Prefecture, the Dojo of Ascetic Training, which means "discipline intended to strip out self-preoccupations and emotional blockages".'

It sounds as though a progression of spiritual consciousness is expected here. Does that really happen, I wonder to myself, or is this simply a romanticised view of the pilgrimage?

'As we enter Ehime Prefecture, the Dojo of Enlightenment,' Mayumi continues, 'the journey progresses towards an experience of greater clarity of perspective. And the last Prefecture is Kagawa, which is the Dojo of Nirvana. Of course, it is unlikely that any one of us will reach this state of high spiritual attainment. But those are the designated stages in the pilgrimage route.'

Well, at the very least, there are lessons I may learn on the way that I can bring back into my life, I muse. I am a lifelong learner, and the prospect of learning new things has always been a prime motivator.

We plan to circumnavigate the island of Shikoku in a clockwise direction. For the most part, we will go sequentially through the temples, in numerical order. However, there will be slight adjustments here and there for greater driving efficiency.

We begin our journey at the north-eastern tip of Tokushima Prefecture on the east coast, afterwards heading to its inland area, then along its south-eastern coast. The route will take us south towards Kochi Prefecture, travelling west along the southern coast of the island, then northwards to Ehime Prefecture through mountainous areas and north-east to Kagawa Prefecture, the smallest prefecture in Japan. I outline our detailed travel route to all the 88 temples in a later section in this book.

In *Japanese Pilgrimage*, recognised as the first book-length account in English of the Shikoku trail, author Oliver Statler speaks insightfully about the circular nature of this journey. Unlike other pilgrimages, Shikoku does not have a specific sacred destination where one arrives, worships and then goes back. As a circle, it lacks a distinct start or finish, meaning the location from which one begins the pilgrimage is not crucial. What matters is completing the entire journey and coming back to where one started, thereby completing the circle.[4]

Our starting point, Tokushima Prefecture, consists of Temples 1 to 23.

Mayumi announces confidently, 'We are all set to visit 17 temples today. The first ten temples are located close together along the Yoshino River valley, so this should be possible. Tomorrow, we will complete the remaining six temples in Tokushima.'

'Let's hope that the weather will hold up,' I say, looking at the ominous clouds in the sky.

But Mayumi's optimism is contagious, and I can hardly wait to get to Temple 1, which is the typical starting place for most pilgrims. However, I now know that Koyasan is the true starting point, based on the weight of tradition. There, one asks for the blessing of the holy man Kobo Daishi. I did not know this when I was in Koyasan two years ago. So I now ask for safe passage and guidance on our trip.

My heart is pounding with excitement.

In my eagerness, I am replaying our itinerary for the day in my mind. In my thoughts, I am already scurrying ahead to our first destination. The anticipation is lovely, but it also takes me out of the present moment.

Half an hour later, we exit the car and hurry towards a busy street intersection. I lose my footing in an awkward misstep. I find myself on the rough gravel with a badly bruised knee and, worse, a wobbly ankle.

The message is both metaphoric and literal. Slow down. Be still. Be present. Experience the simple reality of being-here-now.

Ah. Clearly, the pilgrimage has begun delivering precious wisdom in its very first moments. I take a deep breath. On the slow exhale, I relax and let go. I quiet my heart and my mind. Then I get to my feet and take the next step.

> On the path of expanding awareness,
> I am where I am –
> perhaps more aware today than I was yesterday,
> and still less so than I will be tomorrow.

I had thought **Temple 1: Ryozenji (Vulture Peak Temple)** would be nestled in a leafy pine grove or tucked away in a serene forest glade. Instead, its massive two-storey gate, a dark wooden structure with a weathered look, dominates a lane that reverberates with the sound of human activity. Perhaps the message is to let go of my expectations and allow myself to be surprised.

I am staring at the two muscular, angry-looking wooden statues. Conceived as a pair, these Nio Guardians, also called Kongo Rikishi, are huge, humanlike wrathful figures positioned at the entrance gate (*nio-mon*) of Buddhist temples, one on either side. Their bulging eyes are glaring, their contorted faces scowling. Their stance is bold and intimidating. They ward off evil spirits with their aggressive, threatening appearance and protect the temple grounds from demons and thieves. Their exaggerated features emit a vehement ferocity that conveys strength, energy and power.

I look at Agyo, on one side. He is overtly powerful, with his open mouth representing the vocalisation of 'ah', the first syllabic sound of Sanskrit, meaning 'birth'. Then I glance across to his closed-mouthed partner, Ungyo, on the other side. His latent might is contained in a purposely restrained 'hum' or 'un', the last syllabic sound of Sanskrit, meaning 'the sound of death'. The Absolute is in the space between these two irate guardians, between birth and death. The contraction of 'ah' and 'hum' becomes 'aum' or 'om', the sacred sound of the universe, unspoken yet continuously reverberating.

It never ceases to amaze me that the rhythm of cosmic existence – from birth to death, open to closed, alpha to omega – is encapsulated in a temple doorway.

I have heard it said that a place of worship – like a temple, mosque, synagogue or church – symbolises the heart. In the depths of the heart is a treasure – an Abiding Presence.

The Japanese have a beautiful word, *kokoro*, that, in a way, means heart. But it really refers to an essential interconnectedness, the indivisibility of heart and spirit, soul and mind together. Heart and mind are intrinsically linked. They are one.

Just as the Nio guard the temple with a fierce determination, I resolve to protect my heart and mind diligently against the toxic thieves that are Fear, Lethargy and Negativity. Perhaps this is the reminder I need as I travel this pilgrimage.

For it is said that what we dwell on, we invariably begin to dwell in.

Two white-clad pilgrims throw a quick smile my way as they exit the gate. Though just starting this journey, I already feel a kinship with them. As pilgrims – dare I consider myself one already? – we are bound by a shared experience.

Limping slightly from my earlier misstep, I slip past the scowling faces and glaring eyes of the menacing guardian statues at the entrance gate. I join Mayumi and Katsuji in the temple store behind the gate.

I reach into my black sling bag. I feel inside to reassure myself that I already have what will serve as my most important pilgrim's passport – my beautiful *nokyocho*. This will be my compass, as it were, for this new adventure of going

> The heart is the wellspring of life. What I focus on, I create. For where my attention goes, my energy flows. And what I appreciate appreciates.

from temple to temple. In each sacred site, temple attendants will impress a vermilion seal upon a fresh page and inscribe it in black ink. In eight days, I will have 88 of these stamps in my precious *nokyocho*, proof of my visits to the temples as a *henro*.

I approach a rack of wooden staffs. Feeling the discomfort in my ankle, I select a sturdy walking stick to assist me in the more challenging sections of the pilgrimage trail.

'*Yokatta*. Good. Good choice,' says a shop attendant, nodding approvingly. She eagerly explains that the wooden staff, called *kongozue*, represents Kobo Daishi. It is said that he accompanies each pilgrim as a spiritual guide. She points to the inscription that says '*Dogyo ninin*', which Statler translates as 'There are two of us walking' or 'Two travelling in company'.

This is my first interaction with a local, and I welcome her attention and friendliness with a gracious nod of my head. Smiling, I say, '*Wakarimashita*. I understand.' But at that moment, I just understood the words. I did not grasp until later in the pilgrimage how central the belief in *dogyo ninin* is to the entire journey.

With my wooden staff in hand, I feel an excitement well up within me as I gather the rest of the paraphernalia for my journey. I cannot stop grinning from ear to ear as I flit from aisle to aisle. With curiosity, I survey the different items in the temple store. Mayumi's eyes meet mine. I can tell that she is amused.

I naturally tend to be more conscious of my body language and emotional expressions in Japan. I do this to better connect with my Japanese colleagues and friends and out of respect for a culture that generally seems more restrained.

But Mayumi and I have shared so many adventures that she knows I am truly enjoying this moment. So, we simply laugh together, acknowledging the joy of finally making it here to Temple 1. Ah. Friendship, especially on unfamiliar trips like these, is so fulfilling, so precious.

I take my cue from the mannequin modelling the traditional pilgrim garb in front of the temple gate. I select a white jacket called a *hakui*, going a size up as I intend to gift this to my husband. I settle for a purple stole, so I have a souvenir from our trip. I dismiss the cone-shaped sedge hats as we are not walking any considerable length of the pilgrimage route.

It turns out that all these elements of a pilgrim's costume have ritual meaning. White, the colour of death and mourning. The stick, a grave marker if the pilgrim were to die en route. The *nokyocho* or pilgrim's stamp book, a passport to the next realm.

'In the olden days,' Mayumi says, 'people in Japan were dressed in white when they died. Even today, it is still a practice among devotees. My deceased father wore a white kimono for his funeral.'

It seems like a grim message. The ancient pilgrims came prepared for death.

I think to myself that faith necessarily underpins these journeys. On my journey in life, I have come to know that faith strengthens me to confront the fear of uncertainty. It helps me accept the reality of my vulnerability in the face of the inevitable end to my frail existence.

Mayumi continues, 'There are four lines from a Buddhist poem inscribed on the hat. They are difficult to translate, but these are the same lines that hang over a coffin in a Shingon-style funeral.'

The meaning of the Buddhist poem does seem elusive. Loosely translated, it states that for those in darkness, the world's deceptions are prevalent. For those who are enlightened, there is the realisation that everything is vanity. And since there was initially no concept of east and west, where then is north and south?

I think back to a soul-searching conversation with one of my executive coaches. He asked me, 'How would you want to be remembered when you pass from this world? If you could write your epitaph, what would it say?'

I pondered this deeply for a few days, at the end of which I wrote these lines:

> *A life well lived, a soul who dearly loved*
> *Home in God's embrace*

How I want to be regarded when I die challenges me to make conscious choices of how I should live each unfolding moment of my life. As one friend said, 'You only have so many heartbeats in life. How will you use those heartbeats?'

There is a deeper dimension to this question. For now, though, I brush it aside. I am using those heartbeats right now for this pilgrimage, I say to myself.

Perhaps the hunger to set out on a path such as this is inscribed in the heart. Perhaps there is an inner calling of some sort. We go wherever the journey leads. We see what we are capable of seeing. We hope to catch glimpses of that which we seek.

Coming or going,
all my life's journeys
 a yearning
for that which is home.

Stepping out of the store, I carefully scan the attractive temple compound. Some facts I had discovered in my research before the trip come flooding back. I recall that a Buddhist temple complex is a sacred enclosure that typically consists of several buildings. Each of the 88 temples on the pilgrimage route will likely have two significant halls. The *hondo* or main hall enshrines the principal image or a central object of reverence.

This primary image varies from temple to temple but will be from one of the four main categories of the Japanese Buddhist pantheon of deities: key Buddhas or *nyorai* (enlightened beings), bodhisattvas or *bosatsu* (compassionate Buddhas-to-be), wisdom kings or *myoo*, and celestial beings or *tenbu*.

Within the Buddhist cosmos, there is a bewildering multitude of deities, although Buddhism itself lacks a supreme creator. The array of gods has been influenced mainly by India, China and Japan. Along the Shikoku pilgrimage circuit, 16 of these, including variations thereof, emerge as the main images, with some found at more than one temple.

The other hall is called the *daishido*, or Great Priest's Hall, where Kobo Daishi is honoured. Kobo Daishi then is the connecting thread for all the temples on the route. This cultural hero is the animating personality of the pilgrimage. Many Buddhist devotees, especially followers of the Shingon sect, regard him as a saviour figure in his own right.[5]

There may be other buildings in the compound, such as the temple office, a lecture hall, the head priest's residence, a museum and a cemetery.

In Temple 1, a multi-tiered pagoda contains relics or sacred objects associated with the Buddha. A picturesque pond garden is another charming feature of the compound.

Katsuji, Mayumi and I enter the main hall bathed in a warm, soothing light from the many golden lanterns on the ceiling.

'It is good that we can enter the *hondo*,' Mayumi whispers. 'It is rather unusual to be able to do this.'

I look at her quizzically.

'You might remember that in most temples,' Mayumi reminds me, 'the doors of the main hall are closed. You stand outside, although sometimes you can look through the doors' glass panels or wooden slits. Some temples prohibit photographs in the main hall and the *daishido*,' she continues. 'In other temples, the main image may be hidden from public view or made available for viewing only at designated times in the year.'

I consult my guidebook and learn that Shaka Nyorai, the historical Buddha, is the image enshrined here. *Nyorai*, the Japanese term for Buddha, denotes the highest level of the Buddhist hierarchy. A *nyorai* has reached enlightenment and, therefore, Buddhahood. It is from Shaka Nyorai, the historical Buddha, that all Buddhist teachings have been derived.

Shaka Nyorai preached sermons to his followers on Ryojusen, a mountain north-east of the historical city of Rajagrha in India. People called it Vulture Peak because the shape of its summit was like that of a sitting vulture with its wings folded. Kobo Daishi wanted to bring that sacred mountain to Japan, naming this first temple as Vulture Peak Temple and recreating the scene of Shaka's discourses.

SHAKA NYORAI
(the historical Buddha)

●

Shaka Nyorai refers to Prince Siddhartha Gautama (563–483 B.C.E.), born in Nepal. You may have heard stories about how Buddha attained enlightenment under the Bodhi tree. Or how, once awakened, Buddha had insight into the Four Noble Truths and the Eightfold Path.

After enlightenment, Siddhartha Gautama came to be called the sage (*muni*) of the Shakya clan to which his family belonged. Shaka, derived from the term Sakyamuni, is this Buddha, the recognised founder of Buddhism, hence 'the historical Buddha'.

Statues of Shaka Nyorai show him sitting in a cross-legged position, standing, or lying on his right side (entering nirvana). He is often depicted with elongated ears to denote a willingness to listen to the sufferings of humankind, a bulge on the crown of his head to represent that he is all-knowing and a mark of the third eye on his forehead. These physical attributes are shared by other Buddhas, although they will be in a sitting or standing position.

He has two characteristic hand poses (mudra). In the first pose, he has his right hand held up and the left hand on his lap or pointing downwards. The other pose shows him seated in a meditation mudra, where both hands are in the lap, right on top of left, with the palms turned upwards and thumbs touching to form a circle.

Shaka Nyorai is the primary image at **Temples 1, 3, 9, 49** and **73**.

In these temples, one worships as one chooses. Some pilgrims seem to be reciting a litany of mantras. Others chant some Buddhist scripture in whispered tones or audibly in a beautiful sonorous melody. Mayumi and Katsuji are silent, eyes closed, heads bowed, hands in prayer. I stand reverently, with an open, curious and respectful heart. I pray to the Christian God of my heart, sending a blessing of love and light to all.

Mayumi gives me a quick history lesson as we wander around the temple complex. 'It is said that all the 88 temples were chosen as sacred sites by Kobo Daishi, but historical facts dispute that. That does not seem to matter, though, as he is still the omnipresent figure in the entire Shikoku pilgrimage.'

'It says in this guidebook that it was Gyoki who founded this temple,' I say. 'Who was Gyoki?'

Mayumi replies, 'Gyoki [668–749 C.E.] was a Buddhist priest who lived about a century before the time of Kobo Daishi. He is said to have founded many of the temples on Shikoku. While Kobo Daishi is most revered, Gyoki is also very accomplished and well respected.'

After briefly wandering through the temple grounds, we head to the stamp office to get our first vermilion stamp in the *nokyocho*. This moment is special for me, and I ask the temple steward if I may take a photo of him as he calligraphs my book. He obliges kindly.

He stamps my book with the red ink seal and inscribes it in black ink. Then he sticks a piece of old newspaper between the pages to keep the ink from smearing. From experience, I know that these temple offices may also have a hairdryer nearby to dry the ink completely. I do not see one here, though.

Afterwards, I say to Mayumi, 'Isn't that just beautiful calligraphy?'

Unlike me, Mayumi is not a novice in calligraphy. In the past, she has impressed me with some of her work.

'Did you know that Kobo Daishi is considered one of the three greatest calligraphers of Japan?' she responds. 'The three are collectively referred to as "*Nihon-san-pitsu*". The other two are Emperor Saga and an aristocrat by the name of Tachibana no Hayanari.'

'Oh, I didn't know that,' I say.

'Yes,' Mayumi continues. 'His skill in calligraphy was so exceptional that there are popular proverbs relating to this. For instance, you might hear someone say, "Even Kobo's handwriting contains some mistakes".'

'And is that said to comfort someone who might have performed less than excellently at a task?' I interject.

'Exactly. There's another proverb I like. "Kobo never chooses a brush." People say this when others make excuses for having not done a good job because they say they had bad tools.'

'Aha,' I say. 'I like that too.' I make a mental note to say this to myself as a reminder to be the most resourceful I can be, even when facing challenging situations.

We notice Katsuji checking his watch, and so we head towards the temple exit. Outside the temple gates is a familiar sight – a busy intersection, the car park and, unsurprisingly, several vending machines. In Japan, vending machines are found mostly outdoors, unlike in many other countries. With Japan's low crime rate, they are hardly ever vandalised.

Not only is Japan known for the highest density of vending machines worldwide, but these machines also sell the most intriguing items, ranging from a variety of alcoholic and non-alcoholic drinks to ice cream, soup stock, Pokémon collectibles, shrine and temple amulets, souvenir T-shirts, popcorn, Indian curry and many more fascinating finds.

Here, outside Temple 1, the vending machines carry an interesting variety of non-alcoholic beverages such as water, soft drinks, juice and energy drinks, as well as hot and cold tea and coffee. This juxtaposition brings a smile to my lips – the pilgrimage gives you what you need to quench both your spiritual and physical thirst.

As I go from temple to temple, I learn more and more about temple etiquette. By the eighth or ninth temple, I can go through the protocol of sequenced rituals expected of pilgrims without much instruction from Mayumi or Katsuji.

At the temple entrance gate, I place my hands together in a prayer position and bow respectfully before I walk the pathway into the temple grounds. Then I perform the required ablutions at the washbasin, symbolically cleansing both the inside and outside of my body by washing my hands and swilling water in my mouth to rinse it. I pull back the rope attached to the wooden beam at the bell tower and let it gently strike the bell once.

I light a candle and some incense at both the main hall and the *daishido*. There is a container here for a copied Buddhist scripture or a name slip, also called *osamefuda*. Originally, *osamefuda* were made of wood or bronze, and

> Always and always,
> I awake
> to a world of possibilities
> if I am willing
> to see
> Beyond
> the limits
> of my perception.

pilgrims would nail these on the main temple gate or hall. Hence, the custom of visiting temples was called *utsu*, meaning 'to nail'. Over time and to preserve important cultural assets, *osamefuda* evolved into name slips measuring about five centimetres wide by 16 to 17 centimetres long. Pilgrims write their name, address, age and the date, perhaps even a prayer or a wish, on these name slips bearing a stamped image of Kobo Daishi. I am fascinated to learn that this serves as a pilgrim's identification card to the Buddha and the temple's deity. These name slips also function as a religious business card when given to other *henro* and anyone who offers alms or assistance. Its colour denotes the number of times that one has undertaken the pilgrimage.

Mine would have been white had I decided to purchase some. White is the colour for those who undertake the pilgrimage for the first to the fourth time. But I have neither a copied Buddhist scripture nor a name slip. So I just drop a coin into the slotted wooden offertory box, ring the gong and place my hands together in prayer.

Following this, I go to the temple office to have the vermilion seal imprinted in my stamp book. In Japan, you give things to each other using both hands. So, with both hands, I politely pass my *nokyocho* to the temple steward behind the counter. I say, '*Onegaishimasu*. Please do me a favour.' I prepare the exact change of 300 or 500 yen (roughly $3 or $5) as a donation and not a payment – an important distinction – for the pilgrim stamp. As is the custom, I receive it with both hands when the steward gives it back to me. I also receive with gratitude the *miei* (iconic depiction of the deity at that temple, similar to the holy card in the Catholic religion) from the temple steward or collect it myself at a designated area.

When leaving the temple, I take care not to toll the bell again as this brings bad luck, not the least of which, it is said, is the loss of the wisdom gained while visiting the temple. Upon exiting the temple gate, I turn around and bow again in reverence.

Ritual embodies faith. My time in Japan has deepened my interest in vernacular religion – religion as it is understood, interpreted, practised and lived. These are occasions for me to experience, through symbolism and metaphor, the values embedded in a people's belief. Cleansing with water symbolises the purification of body and soul. The candle flame stands for the brilliance of enlightenment. Incense imparts the reality of impermanence.

Ritual unlocks the power of myth to engender hope and meaning. And it intrigues me to see how these encompass the full range of the senses by invoking visual symbols, sounds, odours and textures to conjure up the expressive power of a particular belief.

I see these temple rituals as an invitation, not an obligation. So, if I wish, I can choose to step receptively into that moment with an open heart, at one with all who are seeking and celebrating hope. Whatever I do, I do with reverence. On one level, engaging in these rituals lends coherence to my experience. On another level, hearing a story from the context of its telling deepens my compassion and understanding.

A low wooden barrier is at the entrance gates of many of the temples we are visiting. This is the equivalent of the bottom part of a door frame. Sometimes it is raised a few centimetres above the ground. This is the threshold, the boundary between the outside of the temple grounds and the inside. Symbolically, it is the entryway out of the secular world full of suffering and into the sacred space of the temple compound.

When the threshold is just a bit higher or slightly wider, I make it a point to mind my step and look downwards, to tread carefully where I need to. This posture is, after all, the appropriate stance when entering the temple. I remind myself that to step on the threshold would be disrespectful, as this would defile a holy place. And so I step over it, careful that my feet do not touch it. It is a subtle reminder to conduct myself appropriately in what is now hallowed ground – to be awake, present, open and engaged.

Inside the temple compound, just past the entrance gates, is a washbasin or a cistern by the side. It reinforces the symbolism of separating the sacred from the secular through ritual cleansing. One purifies oneself before approaching the prayer hall.

While all washbasins serve the purpose of purification, their various designs may carry some other symbolism too. The washbasin in the famous Ryoanji Temple (Temple of the Peaceful Dragon) in Kyoto is indelibly impressed upon my memory. It is shaped like an old-fashioned Chinese coin, the circle representing heaven (yang) and the hollow square in the centre representing earth (yin). Four kanji characters are written, one on each side of the square. Individually, these kanji have no significance. However, one can loosely translate the combined characters as 'I learn only to be contented'.

So far, on our travels today, I have noticed that the cisterns tend to be extended, water-filled stone basins with plastic, copper or bamboo dippers with long wooden handles.

I take the water ladle with my right hand and fill it with clear water – sometimes gently gushing forth from a bamboo pipe. I listen to the water as it swishes, trickles and ripples. I pour the water over my left hand, then over my right hand, watching as it gently slips through my fingers and disappears in the basin in gurgling movements.

Retaking the ladle in my right hand, I pour water into my left hand and bring it to my lips to rinse my mouth, then spit it out outside the trough. I feel its cool, refreshing sensation on my skin and let it trickle between my fingers. I take care not to let my lips touch the dipper directly.

I clean my left hand once more. Then I let the remaining water dribble over the wooden handle I am holding upright, cleansing the ladle for the next person. I empty the dipper and return it to its place.

It is easy to go through the motions automatically. But, as I do this mindfully, I feel my unwanted stresses and immediate distractions peel away. Putting attention to the intention of cleansing, I am inwardly soothed and primed for receptiveness and positivity as though the water itself is a balm.

I have witnessed how the steps in this ritual act are well choreographed and widely practised with reverence. Temple attendants often post illustrated instructions near the water basins to guide visitors on how to perform the ablutions.

As I consult the small route guide with its handy double-page maps, I notice that water is a theme in the many stories about Kobo Daishi. Among the temples we are covering today, for instance, mention is made of **Temple 3: Konsenji (Golden Spring Temple)**, where legend says Kobo Daishi created a well merely by digging his pilgrim's staff into the ground. In **Temple 6: Anrakuji (Temple of Everlasting Joy)**, the story is that, with miraculous powers, he freed a spring by striking his staff upon the earth. People come to **Temple 14: Jorakuji (Temple of Everlasting Peace)** to drink the water and pray for a cure for diabetes. Then in **Temple 17: Idoji (Well Temple)**, the account is that Kobo Daishi provided a water source for the local farmers.

It is, of course, no surprise that water is a crucial element in religions. After all, it is frequently used in rituals of cleansing or purification. To Hindus, all water is sacred, especially rivers. The Ganges is considered the holiest of seven rivers, and each day thousands of worshippers bathe in it as an act of spiritual cleansing. Muslims are required to perform ablutions before carrying out religious duties, and the mosques of Islam often have a fountain or pools of water symbolising purity. In Judaism, the origin of ritual washing goes back to the Torah, and the stories of the Great Flood or the Parting of the Red Sea are often recounted in its tradition. In Shintoism, purification with water precedes public or private worship. In funeral services, Buddhists use water poured into a bowl as an offering to the departed. In Christianity, water is symbolic in many ways, associated widely with baptism. And then it strikes me how significant it is that Jesus described himself as the 'living water' (John 7:37).

Beyond the context of ritual, I have heard it said that water represents consciousness. Everyday language is replete with references, such as 'being in the flow', 'a stream of consciousness', or even 'a flood of emotions'.

> A kinder and wiser world
> begins with a kinder, wiser me.
> So I seek to be cleansed,
> purified and renewed
> that I may bring a more
> loving presence
> and a wisdom of heart to the world.

What is it that I flood my consciousness with? What thoughts do I need to purify my mind of? Proverbs 23:7 springs to mind (aha! a clever pun):

> As a man thinketh in his heart, so is he.

In the silence of my heart, I pray in earnest.

With our tight schedule for the day, we've agreed that we will have no lunch. Instead, while on the road, we dig into the stash of kangaroo jerky and macadamia nuts that I have brought from Sydney. Mayumi delights me with a few Japanese snacks, including Happy Turn rice crackers, described as being 'a little sweet, a little salty and completely addicting'. We pick up our drinks as we need them from the vending machines around. This morning, the drink I select is a can of hot Georgia café-au-lait. It is not exactly a worthy substitute for a nice Australian latte. Still, I have come to enjoy it from my earlier days working in my Tokyo office and when I was facilitating workshops in our global learning centre in Yokohama.

Although we drive from temple to temple, there is often still much walking to do. However, most of the walking so far has been on pleasant stretches of relatively flat ground or short flights of ragged stone steps. I am thrilled to experience only minimal discomfort, even with my wobbly ankle.

That is, until we get to **Temple 10: Kirihataji (Cut Cloth Temple)**, the last of the cluster of temples nestled in the Yoshino Valley. This temple sits atop a mountain, concealed from view. We have to climb an exceedingly long flight of ancient steps to reach it.

It is early afternoon as we start to ascend the steps. Maybe this is where my wooden staff would have come in handy. But I have left it in the car. Perhaps this is one of the moments the shop attendant was referring to when she said, 'You can lean on him. He will support you,' alluding to the wooden stick as an embodiment of Kobo Daishi.

The sun casts a glittering yellow-green shade on the crooked steps, with the light filtering through the leaves of the towering cedars and the overgrown grass. I am breathing hard, yet I estimate that I am only at about the halfway mark of the 333 steps. I push myself to keep going until I reach the top of the stairs. My heart is pounding. My throat is parched. My can of Georgia café-au-lait is long gone.

As though the heavens hear my silent plea, a Japanese woman approaches me and pushes a bottled drink into my hands. I look at her in surprise. All she mumbles is, '*Dozo. Osettai.* Please. A gift.' I glance at the drink – Pocari Sweat. How could she have known this was the cold beverage of my choice?

'*Domo arigato.* Thank you very much,' I manage to blurt out with a bow as I struggle to catch my breath and become more conscious of the burn in my thigh muscles.

'*Osettai*,' she says again with a gentle smile. Then she walks away to join a group of locals by the trees.

This is my first experience of the heartwarming practice of *osettai*, the offering of assistance and support to pilgrims. This wonderful hospitality from strangers shows up in many different forms – giving refreshments or money to pilgrims, going out of the way to provide directions, offering free meals and even a place to rest or stay the night.

Over the remainder of our travels, we will experience other such examples of *osettai*, the living cultural heritage that remains a unique hallmark of the Shikoku pilgrimage.[6] In my upbringing, my parents taught me to give generously, whether in practices of charitable giving, almsgiving or the like. Being the recipient of such generosity, especially when I need it, is a moving experience. I am more comfortable as a giver, I realise. I need to learn to be comfortable with receiving too.

Considering the locations of the remaining temples in our Day 1 itinerary, we make a slight change in the order of our visits. We head from Temple 11 to Temple 17 and then, in reverse numerical sequence, Temples 16, 15, 14 and 13 until we reach the final temple for the day, Temple 12. It is just as the afternoon is drawing to a close. And, for me, that is the highlight of the day – a most memorable visit to **Temple 12: Shosanji (Burning Mountain Temple)**, the second-highest sacred site in our journey.

This is the temple where, according to legend, a malicious dragon had been terrorising the area in the early eighth century. A wandering ascetic vanquished this dragon and founded the temple. However, a century later, the flames from the fiery dragon once again set the entire mountain ablaze, causing tremendous damage to the area. Under the protection of Kokuzo Bosatsu, Kobo Daishi ascended the mountain, subdued the dragon and sealed it in a cave; nevermore did it cause mischief.

At 800 metres above sea level, Temple 12 is billed as the first difficult place to reach in the pilgrimage. Even in the

> **KOKUZO BOSATSU**
> **(Akashagarbha)**
>
> ●
>
> A *bosatsu* or bodhisattva has achieved enlightenment but postpones Buddhahood until all of humanity can be saved. They help others to attain enlightenment and transcend the wheel of life. Kokuzo Bosatsu (Sanskrit name: Akashagarbha) is the Bodhisattva of Wisdom and Memory. 'Kokuzo' literally means 'a storage full of infinite wisdom and compassion'. Also called the Bodhisattva of Empty Space, Kokuzo Bosatsu symbolises the vast and boundless Buddha wisdom that pervades the universe. He is typically portrayed with a sword in his right hand, symbolising wisdom that slays ignorance, and a wish-granting gem in his left hand.
>
> Although a relatively rare figure in temples, he is vital to Japan's Shingon sect of Esoteric Buddhism. It is said that Kobo Daishi's dream of Kokuzo Bosatsu gave him the irresistible prompting to travel to China in his quest for deeper truth. Kobo Daishi is also known to have chanted Kokuzo's 'Morning Star' mantra immediately preceding his enlightenment.
>
> Kokuzo Bosatsu is the main image at **Temples 12, 21** and **24**.

best of times, the strenuous hike up the challenging boulders and rough trails to this mountaintop temple is classed as a *henro korogashi*, a place where pilgrims fall.

Today, travelling by car, the steep and winding road seems to go on and on. The sky turns grey. First a tinkle, then a sprinkle and a splash! The raindrops break their fall on the car window and then shy away. But suddenly the sky unleashes a heavy downpour. The windscreen wipers scramble in a frantic motion. The relentless rain rages unabated. The road is narrow and slippery. I am placing my faith in Katsuji, yet still I hold my breath.

We are rushing to beat the 5 p.m. closing time of the temple office so that we can receive our pilgrim's stamp. There is but the slimmest chance that we can make it to the office before it closes. But Katsuji is determined to get us there quickly and safely. He deftly manoeuvres the car right, then a sharp left, then a steep right again, almost willing our vehicle to fly.

We grind our way uphill, the dangerous edge of the sharp cliffs always just a breath away. I feel my heart racing as we zigzag the severe incline, vast sheets of rain hammering the car. We all fall silent.

Mayumi and I bolt from the car as soon as it screeches to a halt in the car park. We dash across the wet, muddy ground in the long, unforgiving approach to the temple.

Mayumi is a nearly a metre ahead of me and her graceful silhouette in nimble motion guides me through the heavy mist. My heart is pounding in my throat as I drag my drenched and weary body up another two or three steep stone staircases, my ankle protesting in agony. I hold back from calling out to her, '*Chotto matte. Chotto matte kudasai.* Wait a minute. Wait a minute, please.' A prayer of hope escapes my lips from under my laboured breath.

Even with our best and fastest, it is well past 5 p.m. when we reach the temple. The office is still open. The monk sees our wet, frazzled looks and says almost solemnly in Japanese, 'I always close the office at 5 p.m. This time I waited because I knew someone would come.'

Still in disbelief, Mayumi and I stumble over our muttered words of profound gratitude. The monk imprints our *nokyocho* with the precious vermilion stamps. Then he wields his brush for extravagant flourishes of calligraphy. He hands them to us with a gentle smile and then politely but firmly gesticulates that he will now close the office doors.

This outcome is nothing short of a miracle. Anyone familiar with this country will be aware of the meticulous attention paid by the Japanese people to punctuality. It is almost a national obsession. In many a meeting that I attended in Japanese offices, to be on time meant being there a good number of minutes before the agreed hour to ensure an on-the-dot start. Transport officials apologise to commuters if the train is delayed by even one minute. I have even heard it said that in Japan one could set one's watch almost to the second simply by knowing the arrival and departure time of the trains.

I must say that this methodical obsession with punctuality sits well with me. When I was growing up in the Philippines, my father would announce on a Saturday evening to my mother and all of us six siblings the time we would be leaving the house for Sunday Mass the following day. Without fail, he would drive off in our old red-and-black Hudson automobile on the dot. Anyone not in the car at the time he indicated risked being left behind.

An unbridled exhilaration fills the air as Mayumi, Katsuji and I burst into joyful celebration. That we were able to have our *nokyocho* stamped in this last temple on our itinerary for Day 1 is undoubtedly the most gratifying climax of our day.

Mayumi and I look at each other. Her hair is dripping wet, as is mine. Her face is radiant with the exuberance of immense relief. I feel that too, even though the knotted mass of built-up anxiety and tension inside me from our feverish pace has yet to dissipate entirely. I become aware that my face is wet. I cannot say if it is simply the rain, the melting mist, or tears of joy. It must be a combination of all those.

'Kokuzo Bosatsu is the main image,' Mayumi whispers as we approach the main hall. 'He is the wish-granting Buddha, so he granted our wish to come here.'

The main hall doors are closed, so there is not much we can see. But perhaps one does not come here to look for splendour or beauty. One comes here to find hope and feel the connection to the transcendental reality that allows it to flourish in our spirits.

It feels surreal to wander the grounds of Shosanji. Everything is now veiled in a light mist that mingles with the afternoon breeze and drifts down the slope to drape a distant ridge. There are more than a hundred gigantic Japanese cedar trees surrounding the temple. A solitary lantern to the side brings a gentle illumination to the descending darkness.

I wonder why the monk did not close the temple office when he usually does. I am still amazed by the intuitive sense by which he knew someone would come. And what providence it was that that someone was us.

That sense of providence touches me deeply on this, the first day of our journey. This experience has indeed been one of grace in motion, gracious and grace-filled. I echo the psalmist who wrote: 'Blessed are those whose strength is in you, whose hearts are set on pilgrimage' (Psalms 84:5, *New International Version*).

> Hope is a powerful invitation
> to attune my life to live
> in the present
> as if I already know that
> a miracle will be unfolding
> at the end of the story.

When I simply focus on
doing the rituals correctly
and precisely,
they begin to feel forced
and burdensome.
When I do them
unthinkingly,
the movements become
automatic and
meaningless.
But when I put my heart
and mind into them,
the rituals bridge my inner
and outer worlds
and my heart-mind opens.
A simple bow evokes feelings
of reverence, gratitude
and humility.
Cleansing my hands
and mouth parts the veil
between the profane
and the transcendent.
Putting my hands together
in prayer
affirms what I know to be
true –
that the Infinite-within-me
can transform
the ordinary
into the extraordinary.

END OF DAY

MAYUMI, KATSUJI AND I are on a high as we return to the car. We talk animatedly about our incredible experience of Shosanji. 'It was a miracle,' exclaims Mayumi. 'The whole thing was a miracle.'

I wholeheartedly agree. How else could everything have been orchestrated? And for this to have been our last temple experience for the day, what could be more special than that?

'*Omedetou, omedetou*. Congratulations, congratulations,' we tell each other.

'How many temples did we *utsu* – did we nail?' I ask, glancing down at my list.

'Seventeen temples,' declares Mayumi jubilantly.

We have visited the 17 temples in Tokushima Prefecture just as we planned at the beginning of the day. Our time in each temple was limited. But we could linger when we wanted to, and I experience a sense of accomplishment at how much we have done by the day's end. Tomorrow we will travel to the remaining six temples in this Dojo of Spiritual Awakening.

It is a one-hour ride to our hotel. In the rear-view mirror, I see Mayumi's eyelids drooping as she gives in to sleep. Katsuji has fallen silent, too, as he concentrates intently on the road. I drop into a space of stillness and contemplate Day 1, my first as a *henro*.

Undoubtedly, it has been an unforgettable day of adventure with much to take in. There have been amazing sights of temple gardens, pagodas and koi ponds, dark, mysterious halls and old wooden and clay statues, wide-open spaces and thousand-year-old cedars, little shops with brocade amulets, unfamiliar religious and cultural practices, steep climbs stretching up the hills and glorious panoramas at mountain summits.

What has been heartwarming to experience has been the hospitality and friendliness of the locals, especially in the generous practice of *osettai*. We don't speak the same language; we have different social ways and customs. But, deep down, my heart tells me repeatedly that we have so much more that unites than divides us.

This reminds me of previous trips where I met strangers who, in unrehearsed words, shared with me a part of their lives. Like the monk's wife in Chokoji Temple in Hyogo Prefecture who told me that she loved scrubbing the temple floors so they would always look shiny. I was to discover later that the main hall was designated a national treasure in 1954 and the bell tower is an important cultural property of Japan. Or the temple assistant at the Kitaguchi Hongu Fuji Jinja (shrine) in Fujiyoshida City, Yamanashi Prefecture, who, after an earthquake, gave me a lovely postcard of Mount Fuji to remind me that there are many paths to its summit. Or the cab driver who gave me his own umbrella one rainy day so that I would not get drenched while treading the long and winding pathway to the very popular Meiji Jingu Shrine in Shibuya City, Tokyo. Our paths would never cross again, but the moments of our encounter left deep imprints in my heart. I experienced how generosity begets graciousness, graciousness begets gratitude and gratitude moves the heart to goodness and gladness.

In my experience, we are all seeking some measure of wisdom, grace and light. We catch glimpses of these in moments of presence, kindness and generosity.

Finally, my thoughts turn to Kobo Daishi. I am just beginning to realise how he is ever-present in this journey as stories and legends about him abound everywhere, and his statues are given prominence in all the Daishi Halls. Now I understand that it was not just my friend Shin calling him a saint for my benefit but that he is genuinely venerated as a saint by his followers. Who is this man, this Kobo Daishi, believed to be the *henro*'s constant companion on the road?

DAY 2

Legends

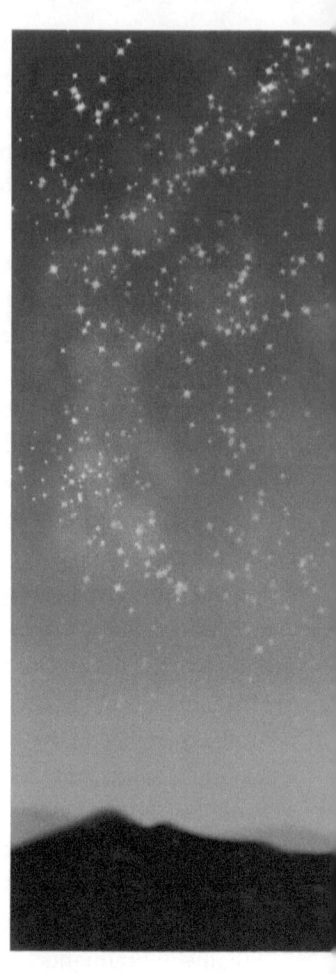

and

Landscapes

T 18 – 23

Tokushima Prefecture

THROUGHOUT DAY 1, I realised that Kobo Daishi continues to endure as a much-beloved figure. More than a thousand years after his death, he remains a central character in the Shikoku pilgrimage and the narratives of its 88 sacred temples.

In every temple and various spots on the route, we see statues of him as a travelling *henro* dressed in monk's robes, with his backpack, begging bowl, walking stick and sedge hat. There are frequent references to him in the guidebook. The primary chant as *henro* walk the pilgrimage is '*Namu Daishi henjo kongo*', which loosely translates as 'Homage to Kobo Daishi'. These words are ubiquitously present in every aspect of the pilgrimage. They are inscribed on the pilgrim's walking stick, stamped on their jacket, printed on their name slip and engraved in temple signages. And I am beginning to understand why.

While separating the man from the myth is difficult, I am curious about the historical Kobo Daishi. So, last night at dinner, I listened intently to Mayumi's explanations and supplemented this with my research. I am deeply impressed by the picture that emerges.

This Buddhist saint was born in 774 C.E. to a minor aristocratic family in a coastal village in north-eastern Shikoku.[1] As a young boy, he was known as Mao ('True Fish'), although the endearment Totomono ('Precious Child') was used more frequently by his parents, Lady Tamayori and Saeki Tagimi.

He left home in his teens to study religion and philosophy in Nara, Japan's capital at that time. Although Confucianism was the widespread doctrine, he was more fascinated by Buddhist teachings. In his twenties, he became a fully fledged monk who continued to search for life's essential meaning.

He wandered Shikoku searching for the highest truths in Buddhism, meditated frequently and sought enlightenment – unsuccessfully on a mountain peak near Temple 21 and then successfully in a cave near Temple 24. For the more significant part of his adult life, he was called Kukai, derived from *kuu* ('sky') and *kai* ('sea'), the two elements that were constantly the view from his cave. In this book, I use 'Kobo Daishi' and 'Kukai' interchangeably to refer to this renowned Buddhist monk.

In 804 C.E. he went to China, where he met his most important spiritual mentor, Huiguo, an ageing sage whose abode was an old mountain monastery. Huiguo recognised Kukai as his successor and instructed him to spread Shingon Buddhism to Japan. So powerful was this spiritual mentoring experience that Kukai returned to his country after only two years, although he had initially planned to be in China for 20 years.

Upon his return to Japan in 806 C.E., Kukai introduced Shingon Buddhism. Its core doctrine is *sokushin-jobutsu*, which compellingly argues that an individual need not wait for death to achieve enlightenment, for this can be attained in their lifetime. This teaching was a significant departure from other Buddhist sects, which believed that repeated cycles of birth and rebirth were necessary for enlightenment.

Until that time, Buddhism's prominent followers in Japan had been aristocrats. The Shingon Buddhism that Kukai brought back from China advocated Buddhahood as attainable by rich or poor, man or woman.

Kukai emerged as a public figure in 810 C.E., when he was made head priest at Todaiji, the largest temple in Nara, the capital of Japan from 710 to 784 C.E. Later, he was appointed to head Toji Temple, the first Shingon centre in Kyoto, which became the new capital of Japan in 794 C.E. and was to remain so for more than a thousand years, until 1868. It is said that the move of the capital city from Nara to Nagaoka (784–794 C.E.) and then to Kyoto was made to protect the position of the emperor and the central government from the strong political influence of Buddhist monasteries. Significantly, Kukai established a private institution that propagated education for all, regardless of rank or status.

Remarkable for his religious accomplishment and temporal abilities, Kukai soon attracted the emperor's attention and gained the favour of the imperial court. Finally, in 816 C.E., Emperor Saga granted his request to establish the centre of Shingon Buddhism in Koyasan.

Kukai passed away in 835 C.E., the same year his mountain retreat in Koyasan was constructed. However, his devotees believe that he remains in a suspended state of meditation, awaiting the coming of the next Buddha, Miroku Bosatsu, who is to succeed Shaka Nyorai (the historical Buddha), the founder of Buddhism.[2] Kukai is believed to be a saviour figure, the spiritual mediator in the time between these two Buddhist deities. It is this fundamental belief to which his followers cling with everlasting hope.

In 921 C.E., 86 years after his passing, Kukai was posthumously granted the honorific title of 'Kobo Daishi' by Emperor Daigo, reverencing him as a great teacher who propagated the law of Buddhism across the country. Indeed, he has been honoured as Japan's most prominent Buddhist saint. Mayumi explains that the title of 'Daishi' ('great teacher' or 'great master') has been bestowed on several other monks throughout the country's history. But the

> ### MIROKU BOSATSU
> ### (Maitreya Bodhisattva)
>
> ●
>
> Miroku Bosatsu is the bodhisattva who saves the world of the future. Thus he is also called the Buddha of the Future. Shaka Nyorai (the historical Buddha) was born 2,500 years ago, and it is said that after the passage of 5.67 billion years from his death, Miroku Bosatsu (or Maitreya Bodhisattva, as he is known by his Sanskrit name) will appear in the world to save all beings. In the time between Shaka Nyorai's death and Miroku's appearance, Kobo Daishi is believed to grant salvation, being the great spiritual light that bridges the two Buddhist deities.
>
> Though it is not always the case, Miroku Bosatsu is often represented as having one finger or hand on his cheek as he rests one foot on the opposite thigh. This is because he is pondering how to save the world.
>
> Miroku Bosatsu is the main image at **Temple 14**.

cult of worship of Kobo Daishi as a figure of devotion has grown so much that the word 'Daishi' is immediately taken to mean Kobo Daishi.

This is the name invoked by countless followers of this great Buddhist monk, whose status in Japan would be akin to that of a saint in Christendom.

After Kobo Daishi passed, wandering priests called *hijiri* came to Shikoku from around Japan to visit the sites associated in some way with him, most notably the ones that mark the place of his birth and where he attained enlightenment. They followed the trails that the holy monk is said to have walked when he was alive, although historical facts show that it is unlikely that he walked the actual pilgrimage circuit. It was these 'flamboyant evangelists of medieval times', as described by Statler, who transformed him into a deified saint and a saviour.

In the late seventeenth century, a Buddhist ascetic named Shinnen published a book, *Shikoku Henro Michishirube*, that outlined the pilgrimage path across the 88 temples of Shikoku. This was a constructed way of linking temples that Kobo Daishi had either visited or had some association with, or sites where he was said to have performed a miracle, rather than a precise route that he had walked or invented. Monks had already been travelling some of these routes. But with the stone markers set up by Shinnen, even ordinary people could visit the sacred sites.

Before the Covid-19 pandemic, the pilgrimage movement sparked by Kobo Daishi used to attract more than a hundred thousand pilgrims annually. In times past, pilgrims set out on the long journey on foot, but the massive development of road travel and transportation infrastructure has revolutionised all that. These days, the majority have, for many reasons, turned to bikes, cars, buses, trains, or a combination of these. Yet, still today, many seek to follow in his footsteps and walk the entire long trail.

Knowing about the historical Kobo Daishi – the name by which he is now best known – I am increasingly curious to learn about the stories that reimagine him as a saint or a saviour figure. It seems every culture learns about itself through fables and myths. Meaningful traditions are passed down from one generation to the next through the stories told and retold, heard and reheard. I smile and think how stories are the currency of human connection, aspiration and inspiration. Myths are great stories that have been told often, heard often and relived in the imagination so often that they shape our human consciousness.

We had a family tradition back in my childhood days. My father, Renato D. Asprer, would tell us stories after dinner while we were all still sitting around the dining table in our home in Baguio City, famously called the summer capital of the Philippines because of its pleasantly cool weather. 'Lesson Giving' was what we called these after-dinner moments. Some stories were about actual people who demonstrated considerable courage, provided exceptional service to the community or inspired others to create a better world. Other stories were somewhat fictional – about a quest of sorts, where there was a hero, smart and strong, who defied the odds and rescued the princess from the dragon, found the treasure or saved the world.

Much like those stories told by my dad, legends about Kobo Daishi abound on the pilgrimage trail. I want to share two that resonate with me now because of the status of women at that time and the status of women today, related to my own experience.

Yesterday, after passing through the entrance gate and dragging myself up that long flight of 333 steps, we reached Temple 10: Kirihataji (Cut Cloth Temple). I had already known that the suffix *ji* meant 'temple', but I learned that *kiri* meant 'cut', and *hata* 'cloth', exactly as the temple name suggested. That is where I heard its origin story. It has many variations, but all versions share a central theme.

Legend has it that Kobo Daishi founded the temple in honour of a lovely young girl he met in a hut at the foot of the mountain. The kindhearted girl gave Kobo Daishi food during the seven days he performed various mountain rituals. On the seventh day, he asked her to help repair his threadbare monk's kimono. She not only patched up his damaged clothes but presented him with a new robe that she had woven from her finest cloth. Grateful, Kobo Daishi wanted to reciprocate her kindness and asked her what she wished for.

She replied that her wish was to become a nun. She told him her story. Her father, a young officer in court, was exiled before her birth because of his involvement in an uprising. Her mother, a lady-in-waiting, prayed to Kannon, the Goddess of Mercy, that no harm might befall her unborn child. Her prayers were answered as she escaped some brewing trouble and successfully fled to Shikoku, where she raised her daughter. Years later, on her deathbed, her mother told her this story and urged her to worship Kannon because of the compassion shown to them. The young girl's story moved Kobo Daishi. He carved an image of Kannon for her and ordained her a nun. She immediately attained enlightenment and was miraculously transformed into a statue of Kannon.

Is it a coincidence, I think to myself, that the main image of Temple 10 is a variation of Kannon? Is this the statue into which the girl was transformed?

I was captivated by this story because Kobo Daishi's treatment of the lowly maiden showed his regard for women. In the Buddhism of Kobo Daishi's time, men and women were not seen as equal. It was thought that women had to be reborn as men to have the potential to attain enlightenment.

Kobo Daishi's teachings in Shingon Buddhism were a radical departure from this. He advocated that every person – man or woman – has a Buddha nature and can aspire to Buddhahood in this life. I could not help but admire Kobo Daishi for this.

That was yesterday. Today, we encounter a tender story in **Temple 18: Onzanji (Temple of Gratitude Mountain)**, our first stop. Legend states that when Kobo Daishi was training in this area, his mother attempted to visit him. However, the temple was off limits to women because of Buddhist Law. She could proceed no further than the gate. Kobo Daishi changed all that. He performed an esoteric rite for many gruelling days, at the end of which the restriction was lifted. His mother was allowed in and eventually became a nun at the temple. In the compound there is a hall dedicated to Tamayori, the mother of Kobo Daishi. In the *daishido* is the image that Kobo Daishi carved of himself. He also carved the image of his mother. This carving, together with her hair, is enshrined in that small hall.

In stories, we often recognise a flash of connection to some situation in our own lives. Like many other women, there were times when I was prevented from making it past a 'gate' of sorts. I was denied a promotion in my early career years simply because, as the general manager of a multinational told me, 'You are a woman'. I risked being passed over for a critical project role in later years for the same reason. In more recent times, I was told at work that it was time for me to return home to Sydney because I had been away from my family for many years while I pursued my career. Those sentiments may have been well intentioned. Still, I could not help but see it as another 'gate' in the corporate world.

It is easy to feel wronged and resentful, but that only depletes energy and creates a story of inertia and defeat. I know that I have burdened myself with negative emotional baggage in these past few months. I need to let go of all that. 'Travel light,' I remind myself, 'travel right.'

I am deeply grateful to my mother, and the thought of her inspires me. When I was building my career, there weren't a lot of women role models. I didn't have a woman mentor or executive sponsor who could help me learn about leadership. But I was blessed to have my mother, Gundena M. Asprer. She was the first female dentist-lawyer in the Philippines. She passed the dental board with flying colours; she topped the Philippine Bar exams. She wrote a book on dental jurisprudence, which became the leading textbook for dental colleges in the Philippines.[3] Not only was she smart but also wise, humble and loving – a beautiful person of faith with a beautiful heart.

I remember coming home one evening and telling her that we had a big exam at school. While I performed very well in the exam, I was sad that I didn't get a perfect score. She told me, 'Yvonne, this isn't about perfection. This is about excellence. Pursue excellence, not perfection. Choose to see what is right in your life, not what is wrong.'

Her words nourish my heart as I stand here in the Temple of Gratitude Mountain. I choose to be grateful for the blessings I have experienced and the gifts that are yet to unfold. I choose to refocus my attention on the things that are right in my life, not on what is wrong. In this way, I choose to create my life's story as one of passion, purpose and possibility.

> We enter the potent dramas
> of myths
> and find metaphors
> to illumine our ways of being
> in the world.

Our journey on Day 2 from Temple 18 to Temple 23 will cover more than 60 kilometres and cross two mountain ranges. By day's end, we will have visited all the 23 temples in Tokushima Prefecture, which guidebooks refer to as the Dojo of Spiritual Awakening. I still do not understand the concept of 'spiritual awakening'. Perhaps it is not so much a concept to understand as a reality to experience. I wonder if I will catch a glimpse of this as we travel this *dojo*.

It is a short, easy drive from Temple 18 to the next temple, **Temple 19: Tatsueji (Temple of Arising Bay)**. It is located in a residential area. This is the first *sekisho* temple – *sekisho* means a kind of spiritual checkpoint that calls pilgrims to assess themselves. Those who have not been faithful to their obligations as pilgrims may find themselves unworthy or unable to enter the temple grounds. Indeed, it is said that those with wicked hearts or minds will be unable to continue the pilgrimage journey. Each prefecture in Shikoku has one such *sekisho* temple.

As I pass the entrance gate, I avert my eyes from the piercing glare of the twin gargantuan temple guardians, Agyo and Ungyo, who I imagine to be scrutinising the pilgrims for any deceitful motives and uncharitable actions. In a way, I am relieved that they tower over me as I would not want to engage with them on eye level. I am not confident that I will pass the test of the Ten Precepts (*juzenkai*) expected of pilgrims. My guidebook lists them as follows:

1. I will respect the life of all living beings.
2. I will not steal and will deal with others with great care.

3. I will practise moderation with regard to sexual activities.
4. I will not tell lies.
5. I will not use exaggerated and extravagant language.
6. I will not speak badly of others.
7. I will always speak truthfully.
8. I will not be greedy and covet possessions.
9. I will not get angry but will remain even-tempered.
10. I will not think bad thoughts.

I am struggling through the equivalent of an examination of conscience and welcome Mayumi's timely interruption. 'I think the idea of Tatsueji being a *sekisho* temple goes back to the legend of a renegade woman named Okyo.'

I vaguely recall reading something on this when I was researching the pilgrimage. 'Could you remind me again about that?' I ask.

Mayumi obliges. 'Okyo was under suspicion for the murder of her former lover. The authorities were hunting her. To escape charges, she fled to Shikoku with her new lover. They mixed with the pilgrims to make it more difficult for the authorities to find them. However, when Okyo ventured to ring the bell at Tatsueji, her long hair mysteriously got twisted up with the bell rope. She could not free herself, so some hair and part of her scalp were ripped out.'

'Oh, that is so gruesome,' I say grimly, attempting to banish the unwanted image from my mind.

'The happy ending', Mayumi says, 'is that their wrongdoing filled Okyo and her lover with remorse. They resolved to turn their lives around, and they devoted themselves to the teachings of Buddhism.'

I glance around the temple compound. The peaceful atmosphere of this spiritual checkpoint is conducive to reflection and invites a rethinking of what is important to me.

What do I need to turn around in my life? I ponder this as I head towards the candle holders. I came to Shikoku seeking some distraction from the disappointments of derailed personal plans and challenges in my transition from Tokyo to Sydney. Is that still what I want, just a change of scene? Or am I wanting some time to reflect, evaluate my current state and make peace with life's changes?

The light of my candle flickers, softly kissed by a passing breeze. I cup my hand around it to steady its flame as the wax trickles down its narrow stem. It casts a faint, unobtrusive light, creating a contemplative atmosphere in the sleepy courtyard.

I acknowledge the universal symbolism of light dispelling the darkness or wisdom illuminating the crevices of ignorance. A beautiful line from the Hindu Upanishads says, 'Lead us from the unreal to the real, from ignorance to illumination.' The light from a humble candle brings the message of wisdom and compassion as it alludes to the enlightenment of Buddha.

Mayumi tells me, 'Did you know that in Japan a lit candle is intended to cast light on one's face so that one's deceased ancestors can recognise you?'

I throw her an amused smile.

In my faith tradition, the lighted candle represents Christ, the Uncreated Eternal Light, changeless and unchanging, the radiance that never sleeps.

I watch how the flame of my candle sways. Gracefully. Gently. Fragile and vulnerable and yet somehow passionate and powerful too. Like the glow of the noonday sun as it commands the centre of the sky. And then slowly, ever so slowly, it fades into the yawning shadows of the twilight.

As I steady the candle in the holder, I bring my attention to the inner light radiating softly from my heart. 'Undim your light, undim your light,' an inner voice whispers gently, prompting me to an awareness of the splendour already within but which, too often, remains hidden and unseen.

It is as though the flame emits a gentle glow. At that moment, I recall the words I long ago committed to memory when reading a collection of Rumi, the Persian poet and Sufi master:

> There is a candle in your heart,
> ready to be kindled.
> There is a void in your soul, ready to be filled.
> You feel it, don't you?

In the temples, we make offerings, like candles and incense – perhaps to seek favour, express gratitude, honour and pay homage. Is it that deities and enlightened beings need these offerings? I should think not. Rather it is we who require some personal transformation. In these offerings is the transformative element that helps make that happen.

I open my heart in prayer and ask for wisdom and guidance to illuminate the shadowed corners of my heart and mind.

I am enjoying our pace today. We are less hurried than we were yesterday. The remaining temples in this prefecture are fewer, although they are further from each other than those of yesterday. I am relieved that we are not

When I embrace my inner light,
I align with the energy of love
* in the Universe,*
seeking to co-create that which
* brings peace to the world.*

rushing, because Temple 20 and Temple 21 are both *nansho*, meaning challenging to reach. They are situated on opposing mountain peaks, with the former at 550 metres above sea level and the latter at 610 metres above sea level.

I am confident the views from these mountaintop temples will be stunning, but I am also somewhat apprehensive of the steep and sharp ascents.

Temple 20: Kakurinji (Crane Forest Temple) has attractive carved statues of cranes and some of the oldest buildings on the pilgrimage. It is said that when Kobo Daishi was training at this temple, he saw a pair of cranes protecting a small statue of Jizo Bosatsu, a well-loved guardian deity of children and travellers. A crane's appearance is promising as it represents longevity and good fortune. He then carved a more prominent statue of Jizo and put the smaller figure inside it. The larger statue is the main image enshrined in the temple.

I look with amazement at the main hall, which is four hundred years old, and the three-storey pagoda, which has stood for nearly two centuries now. I find it incredibly interesting that this lovely and spacious temple is one of the few on the pilgrimage that has never been damaged by fire or destroyed by war. Perhaps there is some truth to cranes epitomising longevity and prosperity.

Seeing the statues of cranes in the temple grounds brings me back to a cherished memory. When our family relocated to Sydney from Hong Kong at the end of 1995, our younger son, John, begged us to put up a Christmas tree. More than just acceding to John's plea, Roberto single-handedly folded all the paper cranes that decorated our tree then and for many years to come. Paper cranes, or *orizuru*, are an enduring classic design in Japanese origami. We did not know at that time what the crane symbolised in Japanese culture. We only knew that these origami cranes adorning our tree were the simple expression of a wonderfully loving man seeking to make our family's first Christmas in a new country one of joy and celebration.

But it is **Temple 21: Tairyuji (Great Dragon Temple)** that triggers an incredible experience for me. This temple used to be the most difficult one for pilgrims to reach, given its altitude and the rough terrain. In 1992, a ropeway – the Japanese term for a kind of variation of the cable-car system – was opened, making it much more manageable.

'Even now,' Mayumi explains, 'it takes more than 30 minutes to get to the temple on foot, even from the car park halfway up the mountain.'

We opt for the ropeway. With a length of 2,775 metres, it is the longest one in western Japan. It travels over rivers and two mountain peaks to this beautiful, secluded temple. This spares us the arduous climb up the steep slope of Mount Shashinzan, though there is still an uphill hike to reach its main buildings.

As we navigate the long approach from the main gate to the majestic temple on a plateau close to the peak, Mayumi says, 'This temple is special. Many temples cannot verify their claim that Kobo Daishi visited their actual sites. However, historical documentation confirms that Kobo Daishi spent his youth on this mountain in 793 C.E. In one of his books, he even mentions how he spent months at this temple.'

I glance around at the lofty gates, buildings and structures sprawled gloriously across the vastly spacious temple grounds and surrounded by old cedar, cypress, pine and bamboo trees. Streaks of mist in the haze lend a poetic atmosphere to the area and the gentle aroma of cedar flavours the cool air.

'Is this where Kobo Daishi reached enlightenment?' I ask.

'No,' Mayumi answers. 'When he was 19 years old, he attempted to attain enlightenment here by chanting the mantra of Kokuzo Bosatsu one million times. He was not successful at that time. But after that it is said that he was able to perform many miracles. He later built a temple on this site.'

The beauty and significance of this serene place move me as we explore the compound. I stroll towards the *daishido*, which is across a bridge in the opposite direction to the main hall. Slipping off my shoes quietly, I approach the inner Daishi Hall, where I stand silently in a posture of reverence.

A mist hangs in the air as a sliver of sunlight slices through the shadowed glaze. I sense all this more than I actually see it. I bow, not in adoration or worship but with humility and respect. My eyes are shut for that inward focus and attentiveness in prayer to the God of my heart.

The staccato rhythm of muted chanting gently rustles the silence, like a breeze wafting furtively, pulling back the drapes of stillness. As I slowly open my eyes, my gaze is drawn towards the direction of that now-familiar chanting sound, stringing together the still unfamiliar words.

I notice the scuffed heels of the woman in a kneeling position a metre or so obliquely to my right. Her wrinkled hands thumb through a small book with the pages folded accordion-style. A sense of mystery lingers in this shallow alcove dedicated to Kobo Daishi.

The soft chanting springs from the woman's lips as though she is muttering, but with urgency. I wonder what she is praying for. Is it for the healing of a sick child, a relationship that needs mending or a loved one's smooth passage to the afterlife? Is it a desperate plea from an anguished heart or an earnest thanksgiving for some unexpected favour?

Many are the shards of fragmented dreams that lie at our feet in our human narrative. For me, this one picture of the woman in prayer is a distillation of the human experience of desire and belief.

In this place of spiritual awakening, to what are we awakening? Or even from what?

Perhaps we are awakening to a fuller awareness of the here and now. Perhaps we are awakening to a calling to a life of purpose or to guidance for a richer and fuller existence. Maybe, awakening will mean faith rediscovered, hopes restored and commitments renewed.

And what about me? What does awakening mean for me? On this very mountain, Kobo Daishi sought to find answers to the questions of life. In some smaller measure, I seek the same in my life. What does awakening mean for me, right here, right now?

The answer eludes me – at first.

Then I begin to recall a story I heard in a philosophy class many years ago. In this anecdote, a man dreams that he is asleep and a hideous demon stands at the foot of his bed. The demon clutches the man's ankles, letting out a most horrific shriek as it does so. In a panic, the man wakes up – still in the dream – and anxiously asks the demon, 'What are you going to do with me?' The monster then replies, 'I don't know. This is your dream. What are *you* going to do with *me*?'

What has grabbed *me* by the ankles, so to speak, I ask myself, restraining my movement, making me uncertain about how to move forward?

My move from Tokyo back to Sydney brought a wave of life changes on a personal and a professional level. Some of these were uncomfortable to navigate. Am I coming, or am I going? Am I being celebrated? Or am I being tolerated? What have I lost? What have I gained? What is it I fear that I dare not see? Whom is it that I cannot be?

It seems as though these changes in life circumstances have held me down, metaphorically speaking, constraining creativity and inhibiting self-expression. I have somehow allowed these negative thoughts to hold me hostage.

I know that what we experience and how we experience it depends on who we are, the point of view we take and the choices we make. As a dear friend and wisdom coach says, 'Our mentality creates our reality.'

So, what thoughts have I chosen to believe? What will it take to let go of these old, limiting beliefs and open my mind to something else, something better?

There is no judgement here – only a listening, a witnessing, a learning.

At this moment, in this place, my awakening is to realise that perhaps the demons that frighten me are those that I have conjured. I may think I am powerless until I remember that I am the dreamer, and I can awaken from my slumber, reclaim the creative power of faith and align with a better version of myself.

Mine are these choices to make.

On this pilgrimage, I see that my journey is replete with metaphors for my life – from the laborious uphill treks to the glory and grandeur atop the mountains, to the rough descents on muddy, slippery ground. There is the obvious and commonplace, the unfamiliar and intriguing, the summons to exploration and celebration. Across all of these contexts, there is the desire to be in control and the inevitable acknowledgement of things beyond my control.

And if there are metaphors for my life, there too is whispered guidance. 'Let go and let God.' Here and now, this emerges for me as a deep inner prompting. It is not a suggestion. It is not a philosophical position. It is an instruction. 'Let go and let God.'

This is the answer I have been seeking. In the context of my journey, this is what the experience of spiritual awakening is all about. I have known this conceptually before, but now the experience on this pilgrimage makes it tangible for me. Let go and let God.

I feel the emotion well up within me, and my eyes begin to tear. I recognise how divided my heart has been. The disconnected parts have created a dissonance that has made me feel that I am out of kilter and have lost my centre, my core. Now, it is undeniably apparent. I think this realisation is the answer to my earlier prayer for the light of wisdom and guidance to dispel the darkness of my mind.

So I surrender all my preoccupations, gather up the divided parts of me and bring them together in an offering to the One who draws all things to unity. I pray for what I want to let go of and for what I want to bring forth into my heart. Inside me, I feel a softening of heart, a re-harnessing of spirit, a re-energising of life with renewed passion, clarity and direction.

The shuffling of steps behind me sweeps away my train of thought and breaks my inner dialogue. I turn around to witness the arrival of other pilgrims.

What I am seeking
is seeking something of me.
I pause
I listen
I reflect
I awaken to my true nature.

I start to inch my way to the side of the hall. I notice that the woman on her knees has not moved from her position. She is still softly chanting, chanting, chanting. Her concentration remains unbroken. Her seemingly altered state in communion with Kobo Daishi is unaltered. I cannot help but respect and be awed by this devotion.

But this time, as I listen more closely, I catch the quick sigh, the subtle halt between words, the lilt of hope in her voice. Perhaps I recognise these because I, too, have sensed these movements in my spirit – from a sigh, to a subtle pause, to a stirring of hope.

I ask that Kobo Daishi send fresh streams of favour and consolation upon the woman still on her knees, deeply absorbed in her recitation of a string of mantras.

With a feeling of sublime gratitude, I exit the prayer hall and step out into the changing light of day. I am greeted by the breeze that carries joy, blows away the dust, plays with strands of my hair and kisses the sky.

I notice that the mist has lifted, and in its place shines a gentle light. Somehow, all this feels like a refreshing breath of hope. Just as well – for without it, our spirits would wither.

We take the ropeway downhill back to the car and then drive to the remaining two temples for the day. Mayumi notices that I seem to be more light-hearted. Even Katsuji can tell that there is a spring in my step. I simply smile, but I know that my experience of 'awakening to inner realisations' in the last temple is the reason.

The enshrined deity for both of the remaining temples on our list, Temples 22 and 23, is Yakushi Nyorai, the Medicine Master Buddha. **Temple 22: Byodoji (Temple of Equality)** takes its name from the belief that Yakushi Nyorai rescues all beings from infirmities, regardless of age or race. And one can easily surmise that Yakushi Nyorai is the main image at **Temple 23: Yakuoji (Medicine King Temple)**. He is said to heal ailments of the body and the mind. I have watched believers pray to Yakushi Nyorai, usually rubbing the part of the statue corresponding to their afflicted area and then rubbing that part of their body.

I seek healing too. The relief of not only the discomfort in my throbbing ankles but also the maladies of greed, anger and delusion that plague my spirit. According to Buddhist thinking, these are the three poisons that are the source of all dis-ease and negative thinking.

I think of all the discontent and dissatisfaction I've harboured in my thoughts and heart, especially in the past few months. More than the healing of my body, I pray in earnest for the healing of my memories.

It is late afternoon, and a gentle rain sets in. We have a peaceful drive to a hotel just a stone's throw from Temple 23. I feel happier, lighter. Perhaps that healing has already begun.

We share stories and laughter over a simple dinner of dumplings and salad, washed down by a glass or two of beer. We toast each other, having achieved what we set out to do – to complete our travels to the 23 temples of Tokushima Prefecture. Katsuji reminds us that we must begin our journey before 7 a.m. the following day as it will be a long drive to the temple in the next prefecture of Kochi. We all turn in for an early night.

YAKUSHI NYORAI
(Bhaiṣajyaguru)

●

Yakushi Nyorai is the Medicine Master Buddha, revered not only for the healing of minor bodily discomforts as well as life-threatening afflictions but also for his ability to conquer vengeful spirits and cure the ailment of ignorance.

Typical representations show him holding a covered medicine container in his left hand to heal mental and physical illnesses and to dispel spiritual confusion. His right hand is raised in reassurance, forming the mudra for granting the wishes of those who invoke him. He resides in the Lapis Lazuli Paradise of the East and presides over the Eastern Pure Land of future rebirths.

Yakushi Nyorai is the main image at **Temples 6, 11, 15, 17, 18, 22, 23, 26, 33, 34, 35, 39, 40, 46, 50, 51, 59, 67, 74, 75, 76, 77** and **88**. Yakushi Nyorai also appears as one of the five main images at **Temple 37**.

END OF DAY

FOR ME, DAY 2 has been a very emotionally fulfilling day. Two days ago, I started this journey, driven by a natural curiosity but without much spiritual motivation. But the experiences of today have caused my heart to stir with some profound realisations. For this I am most grateful. It is astonishing how my Buddhist pilgrimage is creating the space for me to rediscover the God of my Christian faith.

I am sensing that my journeying is becoming more mindful, my travelling more soulful and my wandering more purposeful. And yet there is also a sense of playfulness, enchantment and joy – despite the occasional challenge and discomfort. For, after all, renowned travel writer Pico Iyer himself has acknowledged 'the connection between travel and travail', of wanting to feel and see hardship – both our own and others' – to see and feel the world clearly, honestly, with a better balance of wisdom and compassion. It may feel at times like having to pass through the eye of a needle, as it were, yet through this eye slip the multi-coloured threads of discovery and achievement.

And it is all worth it. I feel that if one is open to the transcendent, there is always wisdom waiting to be gained from every journey.

My outward journeys yet again deepen my inward journeys, aspects of one often mirroring the other. The longing to go out only takes me back in.

Even as my interior world is changing, my external perspectives are broadening. Between our visits to the last two temples, we had the opportunity to spend a brief time at Cape Kamoda. It is a place of scenic beauty located at the most easterly point of Shikoku, the starting point of the Seto Inland Sea. A slightly steep staircase leads up to the lighthouse at the tip of the cliff. Katsuji, strong and energetic, ventured up that headland. Mayumi and I walked along the promenade, looking out across the radiant sea.

So today I have been fortunate to have hiked serene paths that encouraged reflection, stood on breathtaking summits that invited contemplation and experienced the grandeur of the majestic sea.

I think of home, my husband and my children. I think of the elegantly framed artwork on our mantelpiece that Roberto gave me for my birthday a few years back. It is a delicate paper-cutting of 'Desiderata', a beautiful poem written in the 1920s by the American writer Max Ehrmann. In it are the memorable lines: '… be gentle with yourself. You are a child of the universe, no less than the trees and the stars; you have a right to be here.'

I go to bed thinking of these lines from the Psalms:

> When I look at the night sky and see the work of your fingers – the moon and the stars you set in place – what are mere mortals that you should think about them, human beings that you should care for them?
>
> …
>
> O Lord, our Lord, your majestic name fills the earth!
>
> *Psalms 8:3-4, 9, New Living Translation*

I tell myself,
be bountiful with your love,
unstinting with your kindness,
extravagant with your appreciation.
Let goodness, like a river, flow,
for having known the wondrous benevolence
of God, of Source, of the Universe,
how can you be anything but generous?

THOUGHTS

DAY
—
3

Myths

and

Mountains

Kochi Prefecture

IT IS DAY 3 on the road. We begin the early-morning drive in silence, as an initial tentative attempt at a brief conversation is abandoned. We are now on that 80-kilometre drive southwest to Temple 24, the first temple in Kochi Prefecture. This distance is the second-longest stretch between temples in our entire pilgrimage route. Mayumi is her usual cheerful self, though Katsuji seems subdued at the wheel. Perhaps he is quiet because the weather is not so good and we have a long way to go.

And me? I am a touch reticent, if not slightly grumpy, from the abbreviated sleep because of our early start and hunger, assuaged only partially by a single piece of a rather sweet bread called *melon pan*.

Unlike in Tokushima, where the first ten temples are bundled near one another, the temples in Kochi are few and far between. Kochi Prefecture is remote. It is home to 16 of the 88 sacred sites of the pilgrimage – Temples 24 to 39.

We plan to visit 11 temples today – our early-morning start should allow us to do that. Then we will cover the remaining five temples tomorrow. We will need to pay attention to our pace to ensure we stay on track. The temples are quite far from one another, and travelling to all 16, spread over a distance of roughly 455 kilometres, already constitutes a third of the length of the entire expedition.

Perhaps it makes perfect sense then that these temples represent the Dojo of Ascetic Training in the spiritual geography of this pilgrimage. 'Ascetic training' refers to a way of life characterised by austerity and discipline. Exercises and rituals of extreme mortification and strict self-denial are intended to accelerate spiritual development by cultivating an attitude of detachment from worldly pleasures.

My mind wanders, mesmerised as I am by the stunning views of the mountains, sea and sky unfolding before me. At the same time, there is a sense of raw wildness in the rough boulders, the seething and swirling of the sparkling waves lashing the shore and the untamed landscape in the distance. Perhaps these contrasts reflect the fragmentation of my spirit, the longings and the attachments of my heart.

Even my paper map refuses to behave and turns unwieldy as I attempt to unfold it. I trace with my finger the rocky Pacific coastline in the southern half of Shikoku that we will be traversing as we travel west between Cape Muroto and Cape Ashizuri.

I am pulled back to the present moment when Mayumi calls my attention to a pair of dishevelled *henro* in the distance, trudging wearily on the narrow shoulder of the road that hugs the side of the mountain.

On the one hand, I am glad we are making the pilgrimage by car. I can barely imagine the dangers that must continually test their endurance. How do they manage the arduous climbs up the steep mountain trails? Do they have blisters on their feet from hours of pounding the hard, wearisome asphalt? Do they have to contend with any wild animals on the path? Walking the pilgrimage route must really be ascetic training for them.

On the other hand, I cannot help but wonder if we are accumulating any merit, in Buddhist terms, by making this pilgrimage by car. The walking pilgrims undoubtedly merit blessings for their effort, perseverance and sacrifice.

Well, what about the busloads of pilgrims, I think to myself. They are not doing the pilgrimage on foot either.

Ah. Perhaps this is, for me, a lesson in humility – to discipline myself not to judge others but to remain steadfast on my inner journey of patience and perseverance.

Cape Muroto in Kochi Prefecture is just coming into sight at the south-eastern tip of Shikoku. We are about 240 kilometres from where we started our pilgrimage. A rugged mountain ridge slopes to the bright viridescent waters of the Pacific Ocean. On a nearby hill sits a lighthouse.

It is precisely here that the colourful threads of legend, people, landscape and custom are woven together in a fantastic tapestry. At the centre of all this is Kobo Daishi.

Mayumi recounts the story. The young Mao (as Kobo Daishi was then known) spent time living in two caves here, Mikurodo-kutsu and Shinmei-kutsu, and undergoing spiritual training. He eventually attained enlightenment by invoking Kokuzo Bosatsu, the deity who represents the wisdom of the Buddha. He recited the Kokuzo Bosatsu mantra one million times while visualising Kokuzo in the form of the planet Venus, the morning star. At which point, so some accounts go, the morning star entered his mouth.[1] I understand this to mean that the boundaries between Mao and the deity blurred, and he experienced oneness with the Divine in that moment of enlightenment.

Mayumi ends her narration by saying, 'He took on the name Kukai. The English translation is "sky and sea together".' I look around and immediately see the connection. From within the cave, the view of the sky and sea was his constant companion.

I ponder what it might be like to recite a mantra a million times. What comes to mind is a tradition in Eastern Christianity called the Jesus Prayer. The formulaic version most widely known says: 'Lord Jesus Christ, son of God, have mercy on me, a sinner.' This repeated invocation of the name of Jesus Christ may start as a verbal prayer. It can then progress to mental prayer, the invocation repeated over and over again. There is a time, I am told, when the syllables of the prayer become as the beat of the heart, united with one's every breath. When it becomes truly a prayer of the heart, one experiences communion with the divine God.

What an unexpected start to the day. The enlightenment of a holy Buddhist monk triggers these thoughts in me and inspires me to reconnect with a Christian prayer of my youth. I am surprised by this.

I am thankful for the refreshing breeze as we start to ascend the footpath from Mikurodo Cave to **Temple 24: Hotsumisakiji (Cape Temple)** at the hill's peak, an elevation of 300 metres. It is easy to see how this temple takes its name from Cape Muroto, where Kobo Daishi attained enlightenment, and it is not in the least surprising that its main deity is Kokuzo Bosatsu.

Mayumi points out a large boulder that has caught her attention. Several oval depressions at the top of the smooth rock house smaller, almost pebble-like, stones. Mayumi takes one and strikes it against the large rock. Not knowing what to expect, I am pleasantly surprised that the result is not a flat 'plunk' but an unusual sound. Differently sized stones produce different musical tones. Small wonder then that this boulder of andesite, a fine-grained volcanic rock, is known as a 'bell stone'.

It is said that the bell-like sound reaches the 'Other World', adding an air of mystery. It seems most appropriate on this day when the descending mist creates a mysterious atmosphere.

A chill cuts through the air and, shivering, I pull my jacket closer around me. Mayumi and Katsuji also feel this cold blast and suggest we start heading to the car park. We walk briskly downhill.

With the lulling motion of the car as we drive in silence to the next temple, my thoughts turn to the bell stone. All too often, I think, nature calls our attention by revealing something unusual hidden in the ordinariness of the natural world. Then, if we are receptive, nature presents us with an opportunity to discover something about our deeper selves. Looking in that mirror of nature, what subtler aspects of myself am I being invited to reflect on now?

I received a phone call that irritated me earlier in the morning, rendering my words and tone unpleasant. It was as if I were the bell stone, triggered by some external force and giving out a sharp, jarring 'clack'. I could have been more considerate, if not in the message then at least in tone and manner. And though I know that our speech has the power to bless and heal or harm and destroy, in that phone call my words were admittedly hurtful. Caught up in the hurried pace of the day and the ever-impatient mind, I momentarily lost sight of my power of self-restraint. I realise this now, and my body droops. I am penitent. Unlike the bell stone, I can choose to respond rather than simply react.

On life's simple canvas
is painted this powerful truth –
the reality of each moment
is the result of the rich interplay
of both external and internal forces.

Temple 25: Shinshoji (Temple of the Illuminating Seaport), charming in its white-and-orange colours, overlooks the fishing port of Muroto. The temple's name intimates that it has long been dedicated to fishermen. Indeed, local fishermen refer to this temple, founded by Kobo Daishi in 807 C.E., as Tsudera or Port Temple. According to legend, while Lord Yamanouchi of Tosa Castle was travelling off the coast of Muroto his ship was caught in the thrashing waves of a stormy sea, lashed by wind and rain. He was saved from being shipwrecked when Kajitori Enmei Jizo (Helmsman Jizo), the primary image of this temple, steered him to safety. This Jizo is believed to be the protector of fishermen, sailors and anyone else on the water.

The temple sits atop a long staircase. But it is early in the morning, and I am still fresh, so the prospect of the climb does not faze me. However, I am not as fit as I would like to be, and I make the ascent with less ease than I would have wanted.

It is a small temple, the smallest among the 88, but there is lovely vibrant energy here. We enjoy the brief wander around the grounds before we head to the next temple.

It is a quick ride to **Temple 26: Kongochoji (Vajra Peak Temple)**. The level approach is easy until we come to yet another long flight of stairs to the temple, located in the forest at 130 metres above sea level.

Folklore suggests that in 807 C.E. Kobo Daishi drove out demons living in a camphor tree at the temple. Then he sculpted his image in the tree trunk, and that carving is now in the temple's *daishido*. Curiously, on the temple grounds is a memorial tower erected for the repose of the souls of dead whales. Hence, Kongochoji is nicknamed Kujiradera (Whale Temple) because Tosa Province, the feudal name of present-day Kochi, was a town that flourished with whaling.

My admiration for the walking *henro* continues to increase. They endure the rigours of the road, their journey characterised by all manner of austerity and discipline. Even though we are going around by car, I am already beginning to feel the physical strain. I imagine this must be infinitesimal compared to what pilgrims who go on foot experience.

I have not been using my *kongozue* much as we have been going to the temples by car. I have so far managed to negotiate many challenging ascents and descents in the route. However, Katsuji encourages me to bring my staff to **Temple 27: Konomineji (God's Summit Temple)**. This name is not surprising, considering the temple is located on the upper slopes of Konomine Peak. This is another *nansho* or difficult place to reach, situated more than 400 metres above sea level. It turns out to be good advice – I am breathing hard on the climb up the steep incline, and I lean on my *kongozue* to catch my breath. Mayumi is very fit and does not struggle at all with the ascent.

Our efforts are well rewarded by a stunning view of a magnificently sculpted vertical garden. In the temple grounds there are rocks between which flows some water. According to popular folklore, a woman suffering from an ailment saw Kobo Daishi in a dream. He instructed her to drink this water of Konomine (Konomine *no mizu*). Upon waking, she drank the water and received the healing she desired.

There is also a famous story about the devotion of the mother of Iwasaki Yataro, the founder of the Mitsubishi *zaibatsu* or financial conglomerate. It is said that she visited the temple daily for 21 days. Each day, she climbed the temple's steep slopes, 20 kilometres from her home, to pray for her son's success. Her efforts have been well recompensed. I particularly like this story, not just because of my great respect for the Mitsubishi group of companies, but because it shows the immensity of a mother's love.

This is another *sekisho* temple, the spiritual checkpoint of Kochi Prefecture. On the long ride to the temple, the back cover of my route guide caught my eye with its list of 'Seven Gifts Needing No Wealth' (*Muzai no shichise*). To evaluate myself, I prefaced each of the seven items with 'Do I …' and turned it into a question.

1. *Gense* (眼施) – Look upon others with kindness.
2. *Waganse* (和顔施) – Smile at others when you meet.
3. *Gonjise* (言辞施) – Speak to others with kind words.
4. *Shinse* (身施) – Offer to others those free services you are capable of offering.
5. *Shinse* (心施) – Offer your heart to others.
6. *Shozase* (床座施) – Surrender your seat or similar location to those who could better use it.
7. *Bojyase* (房舎施) – Offer your own lodging to others in need.

I resolve to consciously incorporate these practices in my life even beyond this trip.

I look around me. The external environment is so marvellously cultivated. Why not diligently cultivate these seven gifts in the garden of my heart?

It is an hour's ride to the next temple, and I muse on all the stone steps we have climbed since we started this pilgrimage. I wonder how many more mountains we will be ascending today.

Dave Turkington, a four-time pilgrim on the trail, shares that among the eighty-eight principal pilgrimage temples, sixty-one can be found in the mountainous areas, while twenty-seven are situated on the coastal plains. Out of the mountain temples, twenty-five are positioned on, or close to, the peak of their respective mountains, with the highest one standing at an elevation exceeding 900 metres.[2]

For the Japanese, a deep reverence for mountains was birthed thousands of years ago in a way of life that had at its core devotion to the spirits of nature called *kami,* native Shinto gods. Dramatically beautiful, elegantly simple or mythically powerful mountain peaks were seen as the abodes of the *kami*. In the period before the sixth century C.E., the belief was that these summits were too holy, too sacred, and therefore not to be tainted with human presence. Out of reverence for the sanctity of the place, the Japanese people refrained from setting foot on these mountains, lest they provoke some misfortune by an act of hubris. Instead, they built shrines at the base of these peaks and, with pronounced reverence, invoked the deities from afar.

When Buddhism reached Japan's shores in the sixth century by way of China and Korea, climbing the mountains became a metaphor for the spiritual quest, for the search for enlightenment. It was then that people began to climb the glorious peaks, seeking to encounter these deities and to be transformed in some way through these interactions.

With its calm and solitude, the mountainscape offered the ideal setting for reflection, meditation and contemplation – avenues by which the questing soul seeks to experience transcendent reality.

Mountains have their own significance in the other faiths too. In many biblical stories in Christianity, for example, the mountains are places of intense encounters. We go up; God comes down. Personal effort meets divine grace. The mountain symbolically bridges the heavens and the earth. It is the meeting place of divinity and humanity, the sacred and the profane. Perhaps as we raise our gaze to the tops of the mountains that brush the heavens, we are reminded to see the true, the good and the beautiful in ourselves and in the world around us.

I would choose a mountain over a beach any time. I grew up on the northern island of Luzon in the Philippines, in the beautiful mountain city of Baguio, nestled more than 1,500 metres above sea level. Just across from our house was a hill that my five siblings and I called 'the mountain'. It was our favourite playground, the site of many delightful afternoons and treasured memories. I especially loved the brilliant yellow dandelions and the simple white margaritas that dotted our mountain.

'Papa, Mama,' we would call out, 'we are going to the mountain to play.'

I am convinced we were happy on our mountain because of the love, joy and harmony we experienced there. Though I did not realise it then, God did come down and meet us.

On this trip, I see how mountains play a central role in the Buddhist cosmology as many temples are constructed in mountainous locales. And even in relatively flat areas, many temples incorporate endless flights of stone steps as a physical and symbolic simulation of the mountaintop experience. I have always loved the mountains. However, the sharp inclines and the countless ragged steps are now taking a toll on me.

Mayumi and Katsuji warned me at the start of the pilgrimage that a lot of uphill hiking would still be required, even though we were visiting the temples by car. This has certainly been my experience over these last few days.

By the time we reach **Temple 31: Chikurinji (Bamboo Forest Temple)**, it is already past mid-afternoon. I am thrilled that this temple, perched on Mount Godai, is wonderfully expansive.

Gyoki founded this temple in 724 C.E. on the order of Emperor Shomu (701–756 C.E.), the forty-fifth emperor of Japan. It is said that Monju Bosatsu, the Bodhisattva of Beautiful Splendour, told the emperor to model it on the famous Chinese temple Wu-t'aisan (Godaisan). That Chinese temple must have been a sight to behold because Temple 31 is just splendid.

'This is the only temple of the 88 where Monju Bosatsu is enshrined,' Mayumi says appreciatively as we survey our beautiful surroundings.

As though anticipating my question about where we can see this statue, Mayumi quickly says, 'Unfortunately, he is supposed to be a *hibutsu*, a hidden deity, so this statue is concealed from public view.'

> **MONJU BOSATSU**
> **(Manjushri)**
>
> ●
>
> Monju Bosatsu, often depicted riding a lion, is the Bodhisattva of Beautiful Splendour. He dispenses true wisdom that corrects ignorance, banishes delusions and cuts off mistaken ideas, evils and actions. Such an image of Monju Bosatsu is an impressive picture of powerful wisdom that brings joy.
>
> Monju Bosatsu is the main image at **Temple 31**.

Surveying the attractive compound, I can understand why this temple is one of the most popular attractions of Kochi Prefecture. There are stone lanterns and multiple statues, several of which are covered in moss or shielded by shadows from nearby trees. A long main path is nestled in what appears to be a restful nature retreat. The pond garden is magnificent, and the famous five-storey pagoda is impressive, even from a distance.

As expected, I have to climb another flight of stone steps to reach the pagoda, although there are far fewer this time. Despite my physical discomfort and the strain on my ankle, I resolve to complain less about the walking and more consciously cultivate an attitude of positivity, receptivity and gratitude. This inward searching is another element of discipline for me. My intention is to intertwine my steps with prayer, prodding myself over and over to be in the present moment and immersing my mind in the practice of attentiveness and gratitude.

As we enter the gates of **Temple 32: Zenjibuji (Temple of Ch'an Master's Peak)**, Katsuji points to the eye-catching, strangely shaped rocks standing in a row with a green pond in front of them. There is an impressive, fierce-looking statue standing on a moss-covered stone. On the pilgrimage trail I have seen many such figures of this particular deity, Fudo Myoo.

Ah! But this is the one I like the best. The fountain-and-waterfall arrangement provides a dramatic backdrop to this deity. His furrowed brow has grooves like waves. His left eye squints in anger. His lower teeth bite the upper lip, and his braided hair hangs over the left shoulder. The entire representation fits the description of a *myoo*, a wisdom king in the Buddhist hierarchy whose ferocious appearance is a wrathful expression of the central Cosmic Buddha.

FUDO MYOO
(Acala Vidyaraja)
●

Fudo Myoo is the Immovable Radiant King, a deity with a belligerent countenance but a compassionate nature.

The sword of wisdom he brandishes in his right hand represents the sharp awareness that cuts through illusions in deluded and ignorant minds. The coiled rope in his left hand binds those ruled by violent emotions. The flames that surround him, like a cosmic furnace, consume the evil in the world.

He battles evil to bring unshakeable peace and bliss. He cannot be deflected from this duty; hence he is 'immovable'.

Fudo Myoo is the main image at **Temples 36**, **45** and **54** and one of the five principal images at **Temple 37**.

Katsuji confides, 'Fudo Myoo is my favourite deity.'

I ask if there is any specific reason for that.

Mayumi explains, 'Buddhist teachings originated in China, but they are heavily influenced by India. They advocate the idea of a deity protector looking after each of the 12 animal zodiac signs. Many Japanese believe this. Eight Buddhas or bodhisattvas are guardian deities for one or two zodiac animals.'

'My zodiac sign is Rooster. Fudo Myoo is the deity protector of this sign,' interjects Katsuji as he digs into his pocket and pulls out a small amulet of Fudo Myoo to show me.

The messages of wisdom and steadfastness associated with Fudo Myoo resonate with me. These mirror my love of wisdom, inner strength and unwavering commitment to principles and values.

As the day wears on and we visit the remaining temples in our itinerary, I become increasingly conscious of my aching legs and weary muscles. A sense of unease looms like heavy grey clouds from a joyless sky. Again, there is a loud rumbling of thunder, and the rains do not let up. I try to muster a modicum of optimism, but gone are the ebullient energy and buoyant enthusiasm that I felt as we began our pilgrimage just two days ago.

It is only our third day on the road, and already I am sapped of energy, clambering up so many flights of uneven stone steps. Though the views from the graceful summits have been spectacular, the mountains claim every ounce of strength of my being.

Before starting our journey, I was tenaciously focused on completing the 88 temples in eight days. With a weariness seeping into my bones, that cherished yearning has all but evaporated. Was it even a realistic aspiration, I wonder. My leg is limping. But now so is my mind, doubt commingling with hope.

It has been a long day, and I have been struggling to maintain my balance on rigid, unfriendly slopes, with mud splattered on my shoes and heavy rain pelting my tired frame. I cannot even think of the next day or the day after. I can only focus on this minute and then the next, one step down and then the next, moving one foot and then the other.

It seems everything is conspiring to keep me in the present.

The rhythmic tinkling of the small silver bell tied with a silken cord to my *kongozue* plays counterpoint with my uncoordinated movements. I read somewhere that the ringing of this little bell is precisely to pull one's attention back to the present moment. At no time have I appreciated it more than now, when I am carefully negotiating this slippery path. I pause, take a deep breath and gather myself in the here and now.

Then, in this one fleeting moment in time – although it seems longer – I have a sense of the forest opening up to me, moist and vibrant and fragrant. The universe, I tell myself, is benevolent and loving. It is inviting me to walk its paths fearlessly. I feel more assured, more hopeful and a shade braver.

I hold on tightly to my *kongozue*, which has been supporting me throughout the more physically demanding ascents and descents of our route.

Since the *kongozue* is believed to be the embodiment of Kobo Daishi, it must be treated with respect at all times. Mayumi tells me that water is available at the entrance of lodging facilities so that one can wash the base of the wooden walking stick (Kobo Daishi's 'feet') at the end of the day. And even in the accommodation room it is to be given a place of honour.

According to tradition, one has to be very mindful when crossing a bridge, not letting the wooden staff make contact with the ground. This caution has its roots in folklore wherein it is said that Kobo Daishi, while travelling around Shikoku, was once refused lodging and hence had to spend a freezing night under a bridge. The admonition then is not to pound the staff on the bridge so as not to wake Kobo Daishi, should he be resting beneath it.

Using the *kongozue* to steady me as I descend the final mossy steps, I make it to the road.

A true gladness erupts within me, so intense that it takes me by surprise. Indeed, I breathe a huge sigh of relief at having reached the base of the mountain. But I also feel liberated. From what?

The pressure of a future goal dissolved in focusing on the task at hand, which was and is simply to pay attention to the here and now.

It has been a packed day. We reward ourselves with a lovely meal of the area's specialities. We enjoy mackerel sushi served in the unique Kochi way, lightly grilled tuna bonito sashimi (called *katsuo no tataki* in Japanese) and fried moray eel, called 'gangster in the sea' in Japan. Mayumi laughingly explains that this particular eel looks ugly but tastes good. Good food, great company and warm conversation – a delightful way to end the day.

'*Otsukaresama deshita*' is the greeting we exchange – Katsuji, Mayumi and I – as we retire to our respective rooms for the night. This is a greeting so often said that I used to hear it several times a day while I was working in Tokyo. Colleagues said it, one to another, on arrival in the office, during the day in the office corridors, at the end of the day when leaving the office and occasionally before drinks at the nearby *izakaya* or Japanese pub.

The literal translation is a nondescript 'you are tired'. But it is actually a magical phrase that provides an insightful glimpse into yet another aspect of Japanese culture that is deeply appreciative. It really means 'you are tired because you worked so hard' – a genuine acknowledgement and recognition of effort.

I survey my simple room of modest proportions. Pushed against the wall is a narrow bed beside a low stool that functions as a bedside table. Some loose notepaper and a ballpoint pen dribbling a faded blue ink are on it. The bathroom facilities are extremely spartan, though, thankfully, functional. I glance outside the window briefly and note that it is a moonless night.

Spending the night here is ascetic training for me, I think to myself. I am conscious of being somewhat arrogantly irreverent as my humble, cramped accommodation would most certainly be a luxury to those *henro* who have to sleep in much more austere conditions.

Then, I recognise how fortunate I am to be here. Not just in this room, safe and warm, but on this island of sacred mystery. I am grateful.

It is more than likely that some pilgrims will at this moment be hunched up on a bench beside a vending machine, seeking warmth, on the hard concrete or on a rough, exposed camping ground somewhere. Or even, like the folklore about Kobo Daishi, against the solid wall under a bridge.

On that note, I set about cleaning the base of my *kongozue*, which is still damp and stained with dried mud. Still, I have not walked long segments of the pilgrimage, and my staff has remained relatively free of the characteristics of other well-used sticks, such as a splintered base, discolouration due to wind and rain, or sweat marks where the stick is held.

Though feeling spent from the day's ventures, I fix my mind on my experiences of grace throughout the day.

The moment reminds me of the beautiful poem 'Up-Hill' by Christina Rossetti:

> Does the road wind up-hill all the way?
> Yes, to the very end.
> Will the day's journey take the whole long day?
> From morn to night, my friend.
> But is there for the night a resting-place?
> A roof for when the slow dark hours begin.
> May not the darkness hide it from my face?
> You cannot miss that inn.
> Shall I meet other wayfarers at night?
> Those who have gone before.
> Then must I knock, or call when just in sight?
> They will not keep you standing at that door.

> Shall I find comfort, travel-sore and weak?
> Of labour you shall find the sum.
> Will there be beds for me and all who seek?
> Yea, beds for all who come.

I immerse myself in the stillness of prayer and meditation, counting my blessings.

Stillness is the doorway
through which I enter the temple of wonder
just be still and know.

END OF DAY

AS I REFLECT ON the day, I dwell for a moment on **Temple 34: Tanemaji (Sowing Seeds Temple)**, the last for our third day of the pilgrimage. The origin story of this temple is about Kobo Daishi bringing back seeds from China and planting them here. But this temple is also where pregnant women pray for a smooth, easy and safe delivery. By tradition, a pregnant woman brings a long-handled dipper to the temple priest, who removes the bottom. With a blessing, he gives it back to the woman. Symbolically, the woman hopes for an easy birth in the same way water can pour effortlessly through the bottomless ladle. After the birth of her child, she brings the ladle back as a gesture of thanks to Kannon Bosatsu.

I ask myself what seeds I am planting through this pilgrimage. What is it that I am hoping to birth in my life?

I am on an inner journey of realisation. I am on an outer journey of creation. Guided by wisdom and led by grace, I create through my thoughts, feelings, actions and choices.

There are always choices. But clarity precedes commitment. And commitment precedes creation. I find there is a power in being clear about focus and direction. Clarity is what illuminates the path. Sometimes that clarity has a crystal quality. Sometimes it seems opaque or translucent. Whatever the case, it often comes when I sit in prayer or stillness, open to the leadings of the Spirit, my heart-proddings, sometimes vaguely recalling stirrings from way back.

My experiences and reflections on this pilgrimage are planting the seeds for the attention, action and accountability for how I will live my life more meaningfully with passion, purpose and presence. I plant these intentions in the fertile soil of wisdom and gratitude that I am cultivating on this journey – letting go and letting God. I know that when the mind shifts, life shifts. Remove the rock from your shoe, I recall a mentor telling me, rather than learn to limp comfortably. Empowering choices are decisions that design our destiny. I am already beginning to experience this shift towards greater clarity, positivity and resolve.

I curl up under the sheets, grateful I have a bed for the night. Almost immediately, I sink into jumbled dreams of juxtaposed images of countless steps in a place once familiar but long forgotten, where I subdue prowling shadows – perhaps my thoughts and fears in the wildest, most remote parts of my being.

At one point on the winding path up through the dense forest, the tinkling of my little bell makes the shadows recede into the sunlight.

The tinkling sound morphs into the chiming of my alarm clock, rousing me to the early-morning light tiptoeing through the half-drawn window blinds.

The night is over. The dawn lightens the sky. No time to linger or loiter.

DAY 4

Sights

and

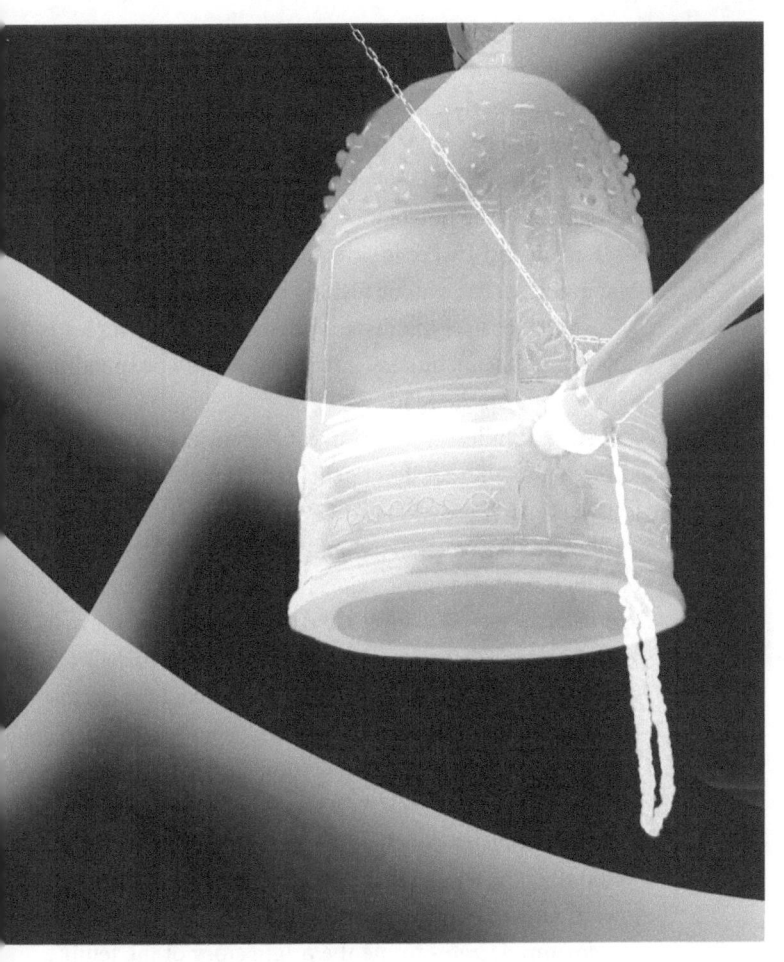

Sounds

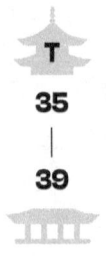

T

35
—
39

Kochi Prefecture

I WAKE UP WELL rested. Considering the tiring day yesterday, I am feeling surprisingly zestful and enthusiastic. It is a day with another early start as we want to make it to Temple 35 for when it opens at 7:30 a.m.

Even Mayumi and Katsuji seem more spirited and joyful as we meet in the hotel lobby.

'Katsuji and I were looking at our schedule for today,' Mayumi says. 'We will be visiting only five temples.'

'That's because the distance between these temples is quite long,' Katsuji quickly interjects. 'We will be spending a lot of time on the road.'

I stifle a smile, but Mayumi catches my expression. She knows I am relieved, if not delighted. This means possibly less walking.

Temple 35: Kiyotakiji (Clean Waterfall Temple) is located on a mountainside overlooking Takaoka in Tosa City. As we approach the temple, I am amazed to see an elevated statue of Yakushi Nyorai that rises even higher than the main hall. It is impressive, and I am not surprised to learn from Mayumi that this statue of the Medicine Master Buddha is now considered a national treasure, a precious cultural property of Japan.

Mayumi points to the statue, saying, 'A businessman in the paper industry donated this giant statue. Thanks to the waterfall in the temple that Kobo Daishi created, the whole town flourished in the paper industry.'

Mayumi narrates to me the origin story of the temple. According to legend, when Kobo Daishi visited the temple in the ninth century, he was praying for an abundant harvest. After seven days of rigorous ascetic practices, he thrust his staff into the ground. This action yielded a clear stream of water that then became a waterfall.

Ah, that explains the name Clean Waterfall Temple, I think to myself.

Though it is barely 8 a.m., several white-clad *henro* are already wandering around the compound.

'*Sumimasen*. Excuse me,' says an elderly Japanese lady who approaches me just as I am about to snap a photo of the imposing statue. '*Henro-san*? Pilgrim?' she asks gently.

'*Hai*. Yes,' I say with a big smile.

She tugs at her white sleeves, smiles shyly and shuffles off.

I am puzzled for a moment and then suddenly get it. I think she is gently reminding me to wear my white *hakui*, the pilgrim's jacket that I bought from Temple 1 but have not worn at all.

'*Gomen nasai*. I'm sorry,' I say quietly.

The practical reason is that it is too big for me, as I had intended it to be a souvenir for my husband. I did not want the additional bulk and weight to hamper me on the uphill climbs. But perhaps the deeper reason is that I do not fully count myself as a *henro* as we are making the pilgrimage by car. For me, the real *henro* are those who walk the thousands of kilometres along this route that is 'merely the string that holds together the pearls on the pilgrimage, the temples themselves'.[1]

Mayumi is convinced that it is of little consequence to Kobo Daishi how we make the pilgrimage – whether on foot or by car. 'He is certain to be with every pilgrim, no matter how they prefer to travel,' she says emphatically.

'You are probably right,' I acknowledge, remembering Kobo Daishi's unconditional vow of *dogyo ninin* – 'we are two travelling in company'. He accompanies each pilgrim on their travels.

Half an hour's ride away is **Temple 36: Shoryuji (Green Dragon Temple)**, a pretty temple with an enchanting triple pagoda and a long stairway leading to the main hall. I am glad I have my *kongozue* with me, as it greatly assists me on these steps.

As we walk around, Katsuji points to another impressive statue of Fudo Myoo, this time strikingly poised against the lush green bamboo forest and a waterfall. Dragon Myoo, a variation of Fudo Myoo, is the deity enshrined in this Green Dragon Temple. He is said to be the guardian of fishermen.

'Does he always look so intimidating?' I ask Mayumi, pointing to the statue of Fudo Myoo.

She says he can also manifest himself in a gentle, affable manner. I must admit, though, that in all my travels, I have only ever seen the wrathful form of Fudo Myoo.

Although the temples making up the entire Shikoku pilgrimage route sometimes seem to blend into each other as indistinct structures, **Temple 37: Iwamotoji (Rocky Root Temple)** is unique in that it celebrates five deities – Fudo Myoo, Kannon Bosatsu, Jizo Bosatsu, Amida Nyorai and Yakushi Nyorai. Another distinguishing characteristic of this temple is that there are 575 individual paintings laid out in a tile format across the ceiling. We have previously come across one or two other temples with ceiling frescoes, but it is somehow in this temple that I pay closer attention to this feature.

The temple invited local artists to add their artistic touch to the panels on the main hall's ceiling. These artists, chosen through a nationwide competition, created images that encompass various objects. It is a curiously curated collection ranging from traditional representations of Buddha and Buddhist deities to vivid paintings of a white cat, bright yellow sunflowers, a Japanese woman in a kimono, cabbages and much more. Perhaps this juxtaposition of various images suggests that the secular and the sacred are, after all, woven into that single fabric called life.

I love the splendid array of colours and themes that draw from Eastern and Western influences. There are watercolour paintings, ink paintings and artistic collages. There is a blend of the holy and the mundane, the cryptic and the fun. There is even a tile with an image of Marilyn Monroe – unfortunately, I missed that and found out only later from someone who posted a photo of that particular section of the ceiling in his blog. I enjoy how these local artworks incorporate a modern feel to this temple complex of old structures.

Then I wander into a spacious room that gives me the strangest feeling. It is as though I have entered a time warp and have been transported into a wildly futuristic scene. In the front of the room is a large four-panelled screen, each panel showing a colourful image of a completely unfamiliar character. Their costumes make them look like sci-fi characters or action heroes from the contemporary world of anime. I don't quite know what to make of it.

I feel confused. Is this a prayer room or a lecture hall? Or simply a place of recreation or entertainment?

It is almost as though I have wandered into a hidden spot in Akihabara, a district in Tokyo that is a well-known haven for electronics and *otaku* goods – figures, toys, hi-tech gadgets related to gaming, manga and anime. I remember how this area in the Chiyoda district of Tokyo, often abbreviated as Akiba, was once described as an urban temple for worshippers of pop culture, geekery and gaming. On a Sunday it becomes a pedestrian heaven, the literal translation of *hokosha tengoku*. Streets are closed to vehicular traffic, and true *otaku* culture geeks revel in their finds of the latest video games, gadgets or cosmetics.

Seeing how perplexed I am, Mayumi comes to the rescue. 'These characters are from a popular comic book, *Hokuto-no-ken* (Fist of the North Star). That's a top-rated manga series popularised in video games and anime.'

I am still confused. 'And these characters are here because …?'

'Oh, they have nothing to do with the temple,' Mayumi says with a carefree laugh. I learn from her later that it just so happens that Kaiyodo, a renowned company that manufactures and retails figures of popular anime characters, is holding a special event in the town as part of a move to revitalise the place. Even the City Hall is exhibiting giant figures of the *Hokuto-no-ken* characters, and the four-panelled screen will be displayed in the temple for a few weeks.

I smile and take a picture of the screen. I make a mental note to send it to my two sons later this evening, curious as to what they will think of it. Rather than feel that my spiritual rhythm has been disrupted, I cannot help but acknowledge that these anime characters bring a contemporary flavour and a light-hearted touch to the solemn temple atmosphere.

I recall a trip earlier in the year to Kimiidera, a temple in Wakayama Prefecture that had over 230 steps behind the entrance gate. As is typically the case, the temple store carried an array of local souvenirs and religious items, including amulets or protection charms. I had promised to buy one for my Japanese friend's young daughter, Mika, and was delighted when I chanced upon an amulet in the design of Hello Kitty, the humanised cat character created by the Japanese company Sanrio.

Hello Kitty is a well-recognised and popular Japanese culture icon that has successfully crossed boundaries and penetrated the global consumer landscape. Interestingly, the Kimiidera amulet showed the Hello Kitty character as having 11 extra heads on her head. This look is similar to the temple's principal deity, Juichimen Kannon, the 11-faced feminine deity who holds the 11 empathic expressions of human existence.

In Japan, Buddhism seems to appeal primarily to older members of society who have associated with temples for funeral services or memorial rituals for ancestors. Perhaps the inclusion in the temple scene of protection charms like Hello Kitty helps modernise the image of a traditional religion like Buddhism to make it more relevant to a broader audience of varied ages and interests.[2]

Ah. Perhaps this is how Temple 37 seeks to refresh its appeal to a younger crowd. After all, pop idols are a cultural form embedded in mainstream Japanese contemporary culture and hugely accepted in the secular space outside Japan. Aren't we all in search of superheroes in our lives?

> Superheroes, the popular culture icons, command our attention and admiration for some time; the real superheroes like Buddha or Kobo Daishi, or Christ capture our hearts and our spirits in enduring, timeless ways beyond the vacillations of time and space.

We are on the road for almost two hours before we arrive at **Temple 38: Kongofukuji (Temple of Everlasting Happiness)**, the most remote temple in the pilgrimage. Located at the southernmost point of Shikoku, it overlooks Cape Ashizuri at the tip of the Ashizuri Peninsula, which elongates into the boundless Pacific Ocean with its blue-green hue. I am told that the weather in this area is extraordinarily temperamental and changeable. Fortunately, today is sunny and bright, the perfect temperature for strolling around the temple grounds. Its sweeping compound includes an assortment of buildings and a garden of pink-tinged rocks beautifully reflected in a large pond.

Kobo Daishi is said to have founded this temple in the year 822 C.E. He carved the temple's principal deity, Senju Kannon Bosatsu, one of the manifestations of Kannon Bosatsu, the Goddess of Mercy. Here, looking out into the sea, he reportedly saw Kannon. So this is the temple from which genuinely devout Buddhists would set sail towards the horizon in search of Kannon's dwelling place, the Land of Paradise.

Kannon Bosatsu's message of compassion resonates deeply with me.

My mind harks back to a memory from decades ago, early in my career in human resources with a Fortune 500 firm. The company held its annual planning conference for the heads of human resources globally. Before one such meeting, to serve as an introduction to each other, the organising committee asked us to submit one word – just one word – to describe ourselves.

On the first day of our global conference, we were each handed a T-shirt upon registration. On the front of the T-shirt, our names were printed below our company's logo. On the back, a single word was emblazoned in big letters spread prominently across the entire width of the T-shirt. That word was the one we had each chosen to describe ourselves. I had not expected such an audacious display of our word submissions.

'This is central to your leadership brand. This is part of your unique story,' the guest speaker declared loudly in his opening remarks as he prompted us to look at the words we had each chosen. A colleague in front of me had the impressive word 'Catalyst'. For another one, it was the corporate-sounding 'Results-oriented'. Another had 'Outspoken'.

I remember how I stood in a corner, practically pressing my back against the wall, in a futile effort to deflect attention from the word on my T-shirt: 'Compassionate'.

I felt slightly depressed. The word seemed to lack the energy of 'Catalyst' or the drive of 'Results-oriented' or the courage of 'Outspoken'.

However, since that event many decades ago, I have repeatedly seen how love and compassion are the essential threads that hold together the intricate tapestry of humanity. As a wife, mother and global leader, I have learned time and time again that being compassionate has enabled me to connect authentically with others. It has helped me navigate the complex dynamics of human relationships, encourage and empower others to bloom and inspire them to contribute to the greater good.

KANNON BOSATSU
(Avalokitesvara)

Kannon Bosatsu, also known as Kanzeon Bodhisattva, is the deity most enshrined as the principal image on many Japanese pilgrimage routes. Called the Lord of Compassion or the Goddess of Mercy, Kannon is depicted in early representations with masculine features but later with attributes of both genders.

In the female form, Kannon symbolises the divine feminine, the divine mother. As the Bodhisattva Who Perceives the Sounds of the World, Kannon can hear the cries of the suffering and take on any of 33 forms to carry out acts of salvation for the afflicted.

Kannon Bosatsu is one of the five main images enshrined in **Temple 37**.

SENJU
KANNON BOSATSU

○

Senju Kannon Bosatsu is the manifestation of Kannon shown with a thousand arms (represented by up to 40 arms, in addition to the two in the centre). The depiction of the thousand arms denotes the various ways those in need are helped. It is said that each arm has 25 divine blessings. Twenty-five multiplied by 40 equals 1,000. Senju Kannon is described as having an eye in each palm and is always watching over us. With great compassion and one thousand arms, Senju Kannon performs different acts to save all living creatures in the universe.

Senju Kannon is the main image at **Temples 8**, **10**, **16**, **29**, **38**, **43**, **58**, **66**, **71**, **81** and **82** and one of two main images at **Temples 80** and **84**.

JUICHIMEN KANNON BOSATSU

○

Juichimen Kannon Bosatsu is the 11-faced Avalokitesvara. Juichimen Kannon is the main image at **Temples 13, 27, 32, 41, 44, 48, 52, 62, 65, 79** and **86** and one of two main images at **Temples 80** and **84**.

SHO KANNON BOSATSU
(Arya Avalokitesvara Bodhisattva)

○

Sho Kannon Bosatsu is a representation of Kannon with one face and two arms. Sho Kannon is the main image at **Temples 69, 83, 85** and **87**.

BATO KANNON BOSATSU

○

Bato Kannon Bosatsu is a horse-headed Kannon bodhisattva. He is compassionate towards animals, especially horses. Bato Kannon Bosatsu is the main image at **Temple 70**.

Before heading to the next temple, which is more than an hour's drive away, we make our way to Cape Ashizuri, which has several other landmarks in the area. Near the lighthouse overlooking the rugged cliffs and meandering ridges is an impressive bronze statue that commands a view of the sea.

It is the statue of Nakahama Manjiro (1827–1898), who was called John Mung or John Manjiro by the Americans. He is the first Japanese person known to have lived and worked in the United States in the nineteenth century. An American fleet rescued him after he was marooned off the coast of Japan. As the only Japanese person who could speak English then, he played a central role in the successful negotiations between the two countries when Colonel Perry landed in Tokyo in 1853 and insisted that Japan open up to the world after having pursued a national isolation policy for more than 200 years, since 1639.

Also in the area is a giant billboard featuring Yataro Iwasaki, the ambitious entrepreneur who founded the Mitsubishi conglomerate in 1870, just as Japan was emerging from isolation and seeking to find its place in the world. It notes his birthplace in present-day Aki City in Tosa, Kochi, his distinguished career and his contributions as a businessman. Looking at this billboard, I feel a sense of pride since my previous company had strong heritage roots and professional affiliations with the well-respected Mitsubishi group.

In the Japanese psyche, the sound of bells is associated with calling for divine protection or keeping evil spirits away.

On the pilgrimage trails, I hear the little bells ringing from the *kongozue* of the *henro* as they walk. Come to think of it, when I lived in Japan I heard myriad bell sounds.[3] The melodious 'kring-kring' from small bells dangling from the bag straps of schoolchildren, the little 'rin-rin' from adorable amulets swinging from the mobile phones of colleagues, the 'clink-clink' of bells on backpack zippers of commuters passing me on the steps of the subway station. I muse with a smile on how all these exemplify the cult of cuteness, *kawaii*, in Japan.

And adding to all the jingle-jangle is a tiny bell in the form of a traditional little Japanese doll called a *daruma* that's chained to my wallet. It was a small present from my son Paolo when he returned from a visit to a temple in Kamakura. Its soft 'tinkle-tinkle' is said to resemble the sound heard when you put your ear to a bamboo cane adroitly positioned in a well. It is meant to evoke the rippling of the water with the whisper of the wind.

Shinto shrines have round, hollow bells (*suzu*) shaped like sleigh bells with a narrow slit on one side. When one pulls on the rope to which the bell is tied, the small metal pellets inside roll around and give a coarse metallic 'rattle-rattle' or a hoarse 'clank-clank'.

It is the end of the afternoon as we arrive at **Temple 39: Enkoji (Emitting Light Temple)**. In the compound is a statue of a massive turtle with a red bib. It carries on its back the bell said to be the original bell of the temple. This likely comes from the story that says the original bell was carried on the back of a red turtle who came to the temple from the sea in 911 C.E. The turtle then made its home in the pond in the temple compound.

I walk up to the *bonsho* or large bell of the temple, recalling that a book I read describes the deep clear tone of these bells as representing the heavenly, enlightened voice of the Buddha explaining his teachings. I reach for the wooden mallet. These bells typically do not have a clapper, so they are rung by striking them with a wooden mallet or a beam. I know that the deep, reverberating sound of the temple bell will carry across the distance. So I do not hit it too hard, to be considerate of households in the immediate vicinity. I get that nice feeling from its rich sound.

At the main hall, I reach for the woven rope to ring the gong (*waniguchi*) twice or thrice, as is customary. I manage to make only a faint, muted sound.

Katsuji chides me playfully, 'Yvonne-san, you have to ring it louder; otherwise, the gods will not know that you have arrived.'

I acknowledge his comment with a broad smile, aware that the gong is used to get the attention of the deities before praying. At the risk of sounding irreverent, it is much like the concept of a doorbell. The reverberating sound of the gong announces one's arrival to the gods.

We are in a playful mood. After all, we have completed our visit to all 16 temples in Kochi Prefecture, the Dojo of Ascetic Training. Tomorrow, we will be off to the next stage in our journey – Ehime Prefecture, the Dojo of Enlightenment.

But first we explore the grounds at a leisurely pace.

There is a serene-looking statue just around the corner. This is Jizo, whom I have come to know as one of the most beloved of the Japanese Buddhist divinities. In my travels around Japan, I have frequently seen Jizo statues by the roadside, in local temples, or on public grounds. One of Jizo's key roles is to care for the children in the afterlife, especially the aborted, stillborn, or lost.

Here, Jizo is portrayed as a monk, devoid of adornments like a crown or jewellery. He has a gentle appearance and a smiling face. His calm countenance conveys to his followers a spiritual optimism that inspires hope, invites trust and engenders compassion.

The Jizo project a certain disarming charm even as they help those under their patronage to transcend the 'wheel of life'. According to folklore, the Jizo take children into the folds of their robes to hide them from demons or keep them safe on their journey to salvation.

There are tales of children who have passed, who, not having lived long enough to accumulate good karma, find themselves in limbo. They must build merit by piling stones into towers to obtain their release. However, the demons come and scatter the stones, so the towers are never built, merit is never accumulated, and the children are never released from this horrible in-between world. In Japanese Buddhist beliefs, only Jizo can save the children.

Just as we leave the temple to begin our drive to the hotel in Ehime Prefecture, Mayumi reminds me, 'Jizo is also the protector of travellers.'

Aha, I think. That would be the equivalent of St Christopher in Christendom. Then I hesitate. On second thoughts, I'm not sure if that is just a myth.

> Ring with joy, o bell.
> Call me to the gladness
> of celebration
> that I may always rejoice in the
> abundance of what I have
> rather than lament the scarcity
> of what I lack;
> I've not always gotten what
> I've wanted
> but I can always appreciate
> that which I have.

> ### JIZO BOSATSU
> ### (Ksitigarbha Bodhisattva)
>
> ●
>
> Jizo Bosatsu, one of the most popular deities, is the guardian of deceased children, specifically the unborn, the miscarried, the aborted or the stillborn. Jizo is also known as the protector of expectant mothers, women in childbirth, children, firefighters, travellers and pilgrims.
>
> Jizo is often seen wearing a red bib donated by pilgrims, red being a colour for expelling demons and illness. The bib represents the parents' desire that their children be safe and protected in the afterlife.
>
> Jizo is also portrayed as a monk with a shaven head, frequently holding a stick with six rings in his right hand. According to Buddhist teachings, a recurring cycle of life, death and karmic rebirth takes place over countless ages. These rings symbolise the six realms of existence, also called the six realms of rebirth into which one is born, depending on one's karma. These include the realm of the heavenly, the demigod, the human, the animals, the hungry ghosts and hell. It is said that by jangling his six rings, Jizo Bosatsu awakens us from our deluded dreams.
>
> Jizo Bosatsu is the main image at **Temples 5, 19, 20, 25** and **56** and one of the five main images at **Temple 37**.

It is a pleasant drive to Ehime Prefecture, where we will spend the night. I am daydreaming. What is bigger, I ask myself, the sky or the sea? I can see the sky in the sea, but I cannot see the sea in the sky.

I muse. Was that a poem I read somewhere? Or did the thought come to me spontaneously?

Suddenly, Mayumi is eagerly motioning for me to look out of the window. What a beautiful sight. In the distance are two glorious rows of colourful windsocks in the shape of koi fish – *koinobori* or carp-streamer kites.

I am used to seeing *koinobori* flying in local neighbourhoods, parks and tourist attractions in Tokyo. But seeing them here in the countryside, framed against the mountain shades of green and rising up against the vast expanse of evening sky, is a moment of beauty. I imagine them in playful banter with the clouds as they dance with the wind.

I feel light and carefree, like a child on a swing. I am oblivious of anything other than colours and sounds and the delight in my heart. I want to sing out loud but instead restrain myself, lest my voice disturbs the reverie. Mayumi and Katsuji are themselves enthralled by the view on the horizon.

Colourful *koinobori* are flown all over the country on the days around the fifth of May, a Japanese national holiday called *kodomo no hi* or Children's Day, marked to wish children good health. Traditionally, it was only a celebration for boys, while Girls' Day was on the third of March. Now, families raise these carp streamers from their homes to honour their sons and daughters and wish them health and happiness.

The carp is a brightly coloured freshwater fish imbued with rich symbolism for the Japanese and the Chinese. It is considered strong and spirited, swimming against currents or even upstream – desirable traits, especially in boys. In Chinese legends, the koi swims upstream through waterfalls and obstacles to reach the top of the mountain. At that point it becomes a dragon, a creature that is an auspicious symbol in Chinese culture. In Japanese thinking, the ability of the carp to climb the waterfall represents achieving success in life.

A thought comes to mind as I look at the *koinobori* in the distance. Their graceful movement makes them look like they are swimming in the sky. Perhaps then I will see the sea in the sky after all.

The beauty of creation,
our common home,
is a portal to the Divine.
I marvel in awe,
I receive with gratitude,
I rejoice in celebration.

END OF DAY

BEFORE I SLEEP, I quickly inventory how Day 4 has been for me. Beyond the sights and sounds on the trail, I have been struck by the beauty of our natural surroundings. The freshness of mountain streams, the lushness of the bamboo forests and the vast expanse of clear sky. What an amazing world we live in and what precious healing balm it offers to anyone willing to receive it.

I feel that I am seeing these more clearly than I have before. I am noticing the shades of green in the foliage, the purple hues in emerald shadows, the shapes of rocks and stones on the ground, and even the sun's rays seem brighter. With fewer distractions, I have become more mindful of the subtlety in what is around me.

I wonder whether this is simply because I am in a new place, with all this beauty. Or is it because I am seeing with fresh eyes, perceiving with a greater sense of presence and appreciation?

I think it is because I have been more attentive to the gifts of the present moment. When I am more attuned to the moment or the task at hand, I find myself in the flow and discover many perfect moments in any given day. Away from the everyday distractions of a hurried, busy life, I can pause and enjoy what is already here before me. Not rushing ahead to the next moment, I can experience the present one. This, I think, is the real dance of life.

I drift off to sleep thinking of the memorable line from Antoine de Saint-Exupéry's *The Little Prince*, one of my favourite childhood books: 'It is only with the heart that one can see rightly; what is essential is invisible to the eye.'

THOUGHTS

DAY 5

Presence

and

Purpose

T
40
—
51

Ehime Prefecture

HAVING SPENT THE NIGHT here in Ehime Prefecture, we find ourselves well positioned for Day 5 of our pilgrimage. Temples 40 to 65 dot this particular geography, which corresponds in this spiritual journey to the Dojo of Enlightenment. Our plan for today is to visit the first 12 temples.

Our first stop for the day is **Temple 40: Kanjizaiji (Temple of Kannon)**, the first temple of Ehime Prefecture. Although it is a quick three-minute ride from last night's hotel, my guidebook says it is the site furthest away from Temple 1 because Ehime is the most westerly of Shikoku's four provinces. Impressive, the distance of almost 600 kilometres we have already travelled. More notable are the shifts I have made in my heart.

A group of *henro* standing on the exterior porch are chanting the Heart Sutra, called Hannya Shingyo in Japanese, its full name being Heart of Great Perfect Wisdom Sutra. It is a short discourse that contains the essence of wisdom. I remember reading somewhere that it was in this temple that Kobo Daishi recited the Heart Sutra to heal Emperor Heijo. I scramble to find my worn-out sheet with phonetic hiragana, the Japanese cursive writing.

Respectfully, I mumble my way through the still unfamiliar recitation, chiming in with the final strains of '*Gyatei, gyatei, haragyatei, harasogyatei, boji sowaka. Hannya shingyo.*' The basic translation, I am told, is 'Gone [or ferried], gone, with everyone to the other shore right now'.

The first time I encountered the Heart Sutra was many months ago when I visited a temple in Tokyo. I received a beautiful pilgrim stamp upon submission of a hand-copied Heart Sutra. I stood by a tall counter, my sheet of semi-transparent paper over the kanji template. I cast a surreptitious glance at other temple visitors who seemed more adept at the task.

Then, my head bowed low, I painstakingly traced the 262 characters in contemplative silence with my calligraphy brush, writing in vertical columns from right to left. My brushstrokes were tentative and uneven. The black-ink kanji were more like sloppy scribbles and scrawls than graceful curves and angles drawn with fluid movements.

But after nearly three-quarters of an hour, my translucent paper bore some resemblance to the sutra template. And my mind did seem calmer. I signed my name, added the date and, with a sheepish grin that belied my sense of triumph, deposited my hand-copied sutra with the temple steward.

At that time, I had not the slightest idea of the significance of the Heart Sutra, the text most often quoted and recited in the entire Mahayana Buddhist tradition, which, among other things, emphasises that all realities, including the ego, are without inherent reality and therefore an illusion. Even now, the meaning of the words spoken by Kannon (Avalokitesvara Bodhisattva) to Shariputra, an important disciple of the historical Buddha, continues to perplex me:

> Shariputra, form does not differ from emptiness,
> emptiness does not differ from form; that which is
> form is emptiness, that which is emptiness form.
> The same is true of feelings, perceptions, formations,
> consciousness.

The teaching enshrined in this text implies the nature of the enlightened mind and the lack of any inherent or intrinsic existence of individual identity, objects and events except in our thoughts.[1] It is a meditation on emptiness. It is not surprising that I struggle to understand its meaning fully. It is said that the sutra, like a koan or Zen riddle, cannot be grasped by the mind. Its meaning unfolds through instruction by a qualified teacher, persistent practice and regular contemplation.

A translation of Kobo Daishi's work highlights the understanding that no matter how extensively one discusses the sutra, the full importance of each sound and word within it cannot be completely articulated. The essence represented by each term is inexpressible, despite efforts by countless enlightened beings to convey it. Given the profound nature of the sutra, those who recite, adhere to, teach or honour it will find relief from their suffering and achieve joy. It is said that by following its teachings and reflecting on them, one can reach a state of enlightenment and acquire extraordinary abilities.[2]

I recall a Buddhist friend assuring me that chanting is less about grasping the content of the sutra and more about focusing the mind. So, here in Temple 40, I close my eyes, relax my body and allow myself to be wrapped up in the mesmerising rhythm of the chanting. I bring my awareness to the spaces between the sounds. The echoes of the chanting carry vibrations of this ancient wisdom. Timeless energy suffuses this ritual space.

As I relax to this rhythm, it is as though there is a blending of the contours of my inner and outer worlds.

We stand in the footprints faded over the centuries of thousands of pilgrims who have gone before us, seeking the sacred and walking the path of age-old wisdom in a place deeply steeped in ritual. Peasants and nobles, priests and hermits, seekers and sceptics – many have come this way, perhaps with heads bowed in reverence and humility. Who was it that said, 'Your eyes and ears can guide you through the apparent, but your feelings and intuition must lead you through the mystery'?

For a moment, or, perhaps, longer than just a moment, I feel like time is suspended. I recall that most elegant phrase of the poet T.S. Eliot, 'At the still point of the turning world … there the dance is.'

After an hour's drive, we reach **Temple 41: Ryukoji (Dragon's Ray Temple)** atop a hillside, approached by a steep flight of roughly hewn stone steps. It is an interesting compound with unusual features.

As the symbol of the hybrid of Shinto and Buddhism, the temple's entrance gate is a *torii* or sacred gate, the traditional gateway of a Shinto shrine. A pair of lion-dogs called *komainu* welcome visitors, rather than the usual Kongo Rikishi. The *torii* is striking in its characteristic colour of brilliant red. The gate consists of two pillars connected at the top by gracefully curved crossbeams, arresting in their elegant simplicity.

Legend has it that Kobo Daishi built a temple in this agricultural area in 807 C.E. when he met a Shinto divinity named Inari Myojin in the form of an old man carrying sacks of rice. People pray to Inari, god of the rice field, for abundant harvests or, in more modern times, for prosperity in business.

The ancient Japanese people saw in their natural surroundings the creative,

> What's at the heart of all, of everything that is –
> God, Source, Universe, Presence indwelling.

harmonising energy of the universe manifesting itself in various spiritual and material aspects of the world. Shinto emerged not so much as a formal religion with doctrines, scripture, institution and founder but rather as a way of life, a view of the world, central to which were the spirits of nature called *kami*.

These spirits were not separate from nature but were of nature, animating the mountains, the seas, the trees, the woodlands and the rocks. Indeed, they animated all elements of the natural world, including the spirits of venerated people who had passed, such as clan ancestors or great leaders who embodied awe-inspiring qualities and virtues.

I remember a discussion with a Japanese friend trying to explain this concept of *kami* to me. He reached for his phone and searched the internet. Then he said, 'Probably the word that comes closest to the meaning of *kami* is "numinous".' I then had to reach for my phone and search for the meaning of the word 'numinous'. My search resulted in 'a sense of a spiritual quality, evocative of the presence of divinity'.

This was Shinto, now called Japan's indigenous religion, the way of life that permeated Japanese culture and imbued Japanese people with a sense of the spiritual even before Buddhism was brought to Japan in the sixth century.

The inextricably close ties between Shintoism and Buddhism, especially in ancient times, are evident in how Ryukoji became Japan's main temple of Inari worship. Unsurprisingly, Kobo Daishi incorporated elements of native Shinto animism into his Shingon philosophy.

The shrine overlooks the temple compound. A bell tower within the temple compound overlooks a beautiful sea view. A telephone booth that seems out of place in these surroundings is positioned prominently beside the bell tower.

Mayumi, Katsuji and I are amused at the sight of the telephone booth, the only one of its kind we have seen in our Shikoku travels. 'If you are in dire need, and the gods don't seem to be answering your prayers, just use the phone to ring a helpline or emergency service,' we jokingly say.

The moment brings a quick recollection. I recall the questions a priest once asked in his homily. 'Have you ever prayed for something and got what you asked for? Or have you ever prayed for something and not got what you asked for? Or, worse, you got something you didn't want at all?'

I remember praying for our second son, John, when he was born with his skin not fully closing over an area of his stomach. The doctors pumped his frail little body with antibiotics because they feared systemic infection. He was to undergo surgery in three days. All Roberto and I could do was pray. I could not even hold him in my arms after he was born because of the risk of infection. So Roberto and I would sit in the corridor outside the nursery and the nurses would bring his little cradle right up to the window. We prayed for him, our arms outstretched in his direction.

On the day of the scheduled surgery, our paediatrician excitedly told us, 'I don't know what you have been doing. But whatever it was, it worked. Your son is completely healed. You will be able to take him home today.'

But I also remember praying earnestly for my father when he had a heart attack at the age of 56. And, many years later, when my mother, at the age of 88, was in the intensive care unit battling severe pneumonia.

I prayed, and God answered. But His answer wasn't the one I'd hoped for. Neither of my parents survived their illness.

I know the pain – my own and others' – the misery of suffering through difficult circumstances or not having that earnest request answered as I had hoped, as I had pleaded, as I had prayed.

Maybe, here on the pilgrimage, I am learning a lesson about how I need to pray. Rich guidance shines through the quote from Marianne Williamson, American author, political activist and spiritual thought leader, expressed in heartfelt simplicity: 'Lord, where would you have me go? What would you have me do? What would you have me say and to whom?'

Katsuji, Mayumi and I are in good spirits as we arrive at **Temple 42: Butsumokuji (Temple of Buddha's Tree)**, our third temple for the day. We are now just past the halfway mark in this circular pilgrimage of 1,400 kilometres around the remote island of Shikoku. Feeling clear-minded and full-hearted, I have a sense of being nourished more and more with beauty and energy, power and grace. It feels like I am growing in my capacity for courage, delight and wonder, reconnecting more deeply with myself.

In these first hours of the morning, the air is fresh and rejuvenating, bathed in the sunlight of possibility, vibrant with the promise of wisdom. Katsuji has started to explore the temple grounds, video camera in hand, annotating his observations for the next segment of his YouTube diary of this pilgrimage. Mayumi is heading towards the stone statue of Kobo Daishi.

As I walk the path towards the candles and the incense burner, I strike up a conversation with another pilgrim making her way there. A friendly kinship develops among *henro* simply by being fellow travellers sharing a common journey. Congeniality exists between us, even on first acquaintance.

In sharing experiences, one becomes a mirror of how the journey has been and a lens through which other aspects of the trip are made more evident. I have always felt that we are somehow interconnected with other people. Still, this pilgrimage makes me think we are so inextricably interwoven, even in the minutest ways, by a power greater than ourselves.

Hailing from the Netherlands, Anika is travelling on foot and by local transport. She is in between jobs and is using this time to clear her mind and reprioritise things in her life. For Anika, the prospect of discovering another country, experiencing novel things and meeting new people is the appeal of this pilgrimage. Though a 'casual believer', as she puts it, she sees each temple as a rite of passage that reorients her focus, centres her intentions and grounds her determination to make the most of the journey. We wish each other well and part ways by the main hall.

On this journey, I have met so many different, interesting people. I might try to convince myself that my life's journey is an individual path. In truth, however, my path is interconnected with that of others. There is much more that binds us together than separates us.

Indeed, a pilgrimage is very much an individual experience, with perceptions and perspectives rising from a sea of personal meaning and understanding. At the same time, an expedition such as this is, in many ways, a collective experience. It is shaped by the companions with whom we make the journey, the pilgrims we meet along the way and the people in the local communities with whom we cross paths. They are all individual threads that come together in a wonderfully woven, colourful tapestry of the lived experience of the journey.

In the quiet of the morning, I bask in the silence. A deeper connection to the Infinite has been unfolding in these last days. I sense the shift in myself from a preoccupation with sheer activity to an open-hearted receptivity.

Mayumi is still at the *nokyocho* office, waiting in the queue to get her pilgrim's book stamped. I am waiting for her by the entrance gates when I suddenly notice a Tibetan monk seated on a wooden bench by the washbasin. His crimson robe is draped around his shoulders. An inner nudge prompts me to approach him and hand him some small bills as *osettai* – a gift, an offering of assistance and support for the journey. He thanks me with a wide grin and eagerly explains that he is just catching his breath and enjoying this brief respite before he resumes his trek to the next temple. He is walking the entire journey and has been on the road for nearly four weeks.

'*Sugoi. Sugoi.* Amazing. Incredible,' I exclaim.

I respectfully ask him why he is making this pilgrimage. With an even wider grin, he says he is hoping it will bring him closer to enlightenment. This is a fundamental teaching of Kobo Daishi, the great teacher to whom his devout followers entrust themselves in their journey towards Buddhahood.[3]

Statler explains that these teachings centre on the belief that enlightenment is attainable in one's lifetime, without the need for reincarnation. This view suggests that everything in the universe reflects the presence of the eternal Buddha. It proposes that humans have the potential to experience oneness with this everlasting essence, thereby achieving enlightenment or Buddhahood.[4]

Here on the pilgrimage trail, I am beginning to understand this more and more. The training of body, mind and speech is ingrained in the comforting solace of rituals involved in the pilgrim's journey. Walking the pilgrimage is a body ritual that demonstrates their earnest efforts. Turning their minds to meditation as they walk is a ritual that centres their intentions and keeps them focused on the spirit of their journey. The chanting of mantras in the temple is a ritual relating to speech. Indeed, there is a rich kaleidoscope of faith and religiosity beneath the exteriors.

As the monk bids farewell and prepares to set off on the next part of his journey, I wish him all the best. The task of the devotees is to perform these rituals to the best of their ability. They entrust their enlightenment to Kobo Daishi, whose help they invoke with their continual chants of '*Namu Daishi henjo kongo.* Homage to Kobo Daishi.' The pilgrim monk has taken all this to heart.

We come from different faiths, but I cannot help but feel we share a common spiritual bond despite our divergent paths. We are both wayfarers seeking a deeper connection to the truest essence of ourselves.

On the way to **Temple 43: Meisekiji (Brilliant Stone Temple)**, I say to Mayumi, 'Maybe I will wear my *hakui*,' thinking of the encounter I had with the elderly Japanese woman yesterday.

'Yes,' Katsuji enthuses. 'Wear it. You will look like a real *henro*.'

So I open my suitcase when we are in the car park and don my *hakui* for the first time since the pilgrimage started.

It feels too big for me, though. Even as Katsuji is voicing his approval, I allow him to take only one photo of me in this oversized jacket.

Returning to the car after visiting the temple, I announce to Mayumi and Katsuji as I fold my *hakui* and place it back into my suitcase, 'Well, I've worn it once now. That was it. The next time I pull this out of my suitcase will be in Sydney when I give it to my husband.' We all laugh together.

Now I know why I am not wearing the pilgrim jacket on this journey. It is because of vanity, I chide myself silently. That's not a very encouraging thought, considering we are in the Dojo of Enlightenment.

Temple 44: Daihoji (Great Treasure Temple) stands on forested ground in an area known as the Kuma Highland. Kuma was the name of a woman who begged Kobo Daishi for assistance in the early ninth century because the barren land in the area was hostile to growing crops. He altered the river's course to bring it closer to the temple, thereby providing the irrigation required to make the land more fertile. That he was able to do this speaks to his outstanding engineering

Like so many others,
I am on this pilgrimage as a seeker
who explores the spiritual path of the heart –
not as a nomad wandering aimlessly,
but as one who believes the Truth as revealed
and journeys towards Source.

skills and his deep humanity. With an accessible water source to make crops grow, farmers returned to the area.

I stop and think. What is it that makes life sacred and meaningful? To me, one important aspect is how I use my talents and best gifts to make a difference in the lives of others. Perhaps that is why this story of Kobo Daishi speaks to me as it does. I am convinced that the Divine comes through our hands, our minds, our hearts. Our talents are both an awesome gift and a tremendous responsibility.

My reverie is broken as I see hanging on the entrance gates of the temple beautiful giant straw sandals called *owaraji*. The *waraji* are traditional sandals woven from rice-straw rope. The honorific prefix '*o*' is used in this instance to mean 'huge, gigantic, big'.

As I stare at them, Mayumi says, 'As you know, *owaraji* by the temple gates act as a charm against evil. Their huge size symbolises the power and might of the deities who are the guardians of the temple.'

I smile to myself as I am reminded of my friend in Singapore who lives alone but always puts two pairs of large-sized men's shoes outside the entrance to her apartment to deter any would-be intruders.

Mayumi continues, 'In olden times, the *waraji* worn by the common people did not last very long because dirt and soil from the rough, unpaved roads filled the soles of the straw sandals. So people would hang a spare pair of *waraji* on their belts in case they needed to urgently replace their worn ones. The samurai, those elite warriors in feudal Japan known for their deft and quick movements, also wore this type of footwear.'

I am amused as she reveals another titbit of information: 'Interestingly, in old pictures, even horses are shown as wearing *waraji*.'

As Mayumi walks on, I recollect a memorable day in October 2018 when my friend Kumi and I were visiting Sensoji Temple in Asakusa, Tokyo. On that day, the temple's old *owaraji* were due to be taken down and replaced with a brand-new pair, an event that happens roughly every ten years. I was all eyes as one of the largest pairs of *owaraji* in Japan – each straw sandal measuring 4.5 metres in length, 1.5 metres in width and weighing almost 500 kilograms – was hung on the temple's Hozomon gate.

Having been present at that special ceremony in Sensoji Temple, I have an even greater appreciation of the symbolism of the *owaraji* that I have now seen by several temple entrance gates here in Shikoku.

From experience, I know that people touch these *owaraji* to pray for healthy, sturdy feet and the endurance to walk long distances without injury. In some other temples, *henro* donate regular-sized straw sandals as an offering for having recovered from diseases of the legs or feet. In the temple shops, one can also buy miniature *waraji* talismans for relief from foot pain or protection from injuries to the lower extremities. I remain sceptical that touching the *owaraji* can ease the pain in one's ankles. Nevertheless, I help Mayumi choose the pair of miniature *waraji* to buy for her mother. I consider buying one to hang on my backpack too.

In my view, human nature is such that we all seek relief from various afflictions and sufferings in our earthly existence.

On this footpath of life,
I stand side by side with friends,
in conversations heart to heart,
as we explore step by step
new and more fulfilling
ways of being.

Regardless of our religious orientation, we intuitively turn to some transcendent mystical reality for comfort.

Undoubtedly, a highlight of the day is the unforgettable visit to the awe-inspiring **Temple 45: Iwayaji (Rock Cave Temple)**, the fourth-highest temple on the pilgrimage trail.

I have always felt that mountains are fascinating and mysterious. In my experience, they draw us, inspire awe, touch the depths of our being and uplift our spirits. It is as though mountains symbolise our loftiest aspirations of heart and mind; they quicken our striving for what lies above.

It is said that Kobo Daishi built a temple on this site presented to him by a mysterious priestess. He also carved two statues of Fudo Myoo as the main image, one of stone and one of wood. The statue fashioned from stone was positioned in a cave behind the temple. The one in wood was enshrined in the main hall. With the stone image of Fudo Myoo in the cave, the entire mountain became a sacred place, an object of worship. Indeed, here in Iwayaji, the mountain is the main deity, conducting symphonies of colour and sound in this glorious theatre of nature rising straight up into the sky.

Concrete paths and rough stone steps find their place among the mossy rocks in the gently sloping forests. My eyes strain to trace the tops of the majestic trees that salute the heavens with their canopies of green leaves. A beautifully carved wooden structure greets pilgrims as they begin the uphill climb of a steep 700-metre approach from the temple entrance to the main hall.

This temple in Ehime Prefecture is *henro korogashi*, considered among the most challenging spots to reach in the Shikoku pilgrimage because of the arduous trek up the steep mountainside. It is with extreme trepidation that I view the laborious ascent.

My trepidation is put to shame at the sight of two elderly Japanese pilgrims determinedly climbing the long stone staircases. 'If they can do it, I can do it too,' I whisper to myself.

I stop to catch my breath on the ever-steepening track. As I climb the stone path, the descending pilgrims see me leaning on my *kongozue*, a trudging weariness in my heavy-footed step. They prod me on with cheers of '*Gambatte. Gambatte kudasai*.' This can be loosely translated as 'Please do your best', 'Don't give up' or 'Hang in there'.

The words take me back to another challenging time when I was a newcomer to Japan, overwhelmed by the culture and the job ahead of me. Now, the words energise me again to believe in my ability to achieve my goal. This popular expression reflects the admirable attitude and spirit of perseverance, determination and comradeship deeply rooted in the Japanese psyche and philosophy of life.

Their encouragement fuels my resolve to forge ahead slowly but steadily. '*Gambarimasu*,' I call back bravely, using a variant of the original word that indicates that I will continue to persevere and press on, enduring whatever hardship I encounter so as to reach the top of the mountain.

I tend to make up rhymes when I go out walking alone. And at that very moment a mantra spontaneously takes shape firmly within me. I utter it under my breath:

> The paths are hard. The paths are long.
> Put one foot in front of the other and move along.

> No more asking, 'When will I get to the end of the path?'
> To simply move forward is enough.

I resolutely connect to the heartbeat of the words. Now I am moving to a slow but steady internal rhythm.

I triumphantly pass the ancient stone statues lining the trail, some with faces half bitten off or foreheads weathered and beaten. I imagine sharing the footpath with these woodland gods who cheer me on with an eager '*Gambatte!*' even as they watch pilgrim after pilgrim make the demanding ascent. The stone statues stand at attention and keep me company for a couple of hundred metres at least until the temple finally comes into sight.

It is nestled at the base of a huge rockface. A rickety-looking wooden ladder is precariously perched against the larger of the two prominent indentations in the deep clefts of the cliff. I watch a few pilgrims go boldly up the ladder and gingerly walk the narrow platform in the aperture that gives them a commanding sweep of the entire temple complex and the valley below. Then they briefly venture into a small alcove. Little wonder the English name of this temple is Rock Cave Temple.

I look at the angle of the ladder and weigh the challenge of the descent against the ascent. I err on the side of prudence and decide to give the ladder a miss. I cheer Mayumi on as she climbs the ladder. She waves back to me when she reaches the top.

There is much to explore in the temple grounds, including an ominous-looking cave behind the main hall. I walk down some uneven steps into the earth 10 metres deep, edging my way forward even as I begin to search the shadows for familiar outlines. The darkened interior reveals burned candles and flower offerings to stone-carved statues on rock-like altars. I peer into the dimness and recognise a large stone statue of Kobo Daishi in this warm harbour in the earth. My heart beats more quickly, but I do not know if it is because I am feeling hemmed in by the dark, cramped space or because there truly is some sense of the sacred here.

Exiting the dark cave, I turn to contemplate my surroundings, my view from the mountaintop stretching over hundreds of kilometres. It is a magnificent vista, with the rocky cliff jutting into the sky, the sprawling temple complex with mysterious caves and wooden structures, and the serene valley below. This mountain temple is truly a highlight of the journey and a cherished experience. I feel as though my heart is soaring, reaching above the massive cedars to touch the sunlit dome of heaven.

Completing the arduous ascent is a metaphor for how my potential lies beyond my comfort zone. It is within my reach if I am willing to stretch, really stretch towards it. I know from experience that my potential is always greater than how I see it or what I believe it to be. Once again, that is affirmed in both a physical and a spiritual way. I resolve to press on graciously and gracefully beyond my imagined limits. The famous words of the poet Robert Browning come to the fore: 'Ah, but a man's reach should exceed his grasp, / Or what's a heaven for?'

I'm finally learning
the choreography of pilgrimage –
one foot forward and then the other;
and no matter the ascent or the descent,
be present, stay centred and keep going.
Oh, yes, and enjoy the journey.
Joyfully catch the rhythm for the dance of life.

Exciting discoveries unfold in the remainder of the temples we visit today. But, to me, it now feels a bit anticlimactic.

Temple 46: Joruriji (Pure Emerald Temple) is surrounded by junipers said to be a thousand years old. Buddha's footprints are imprinted on the ground. Apparently, all tiredness and aches will disappear if you stand on these with bare feet. With an air of bravado, I skip this, however, as I am feeling a new sense of confidence and sure-footedness. Triumphant at my scaling of the difficult path up to Temple 45, I am now certain I have the energy to go out and conquer the world. Success at accomplishing what I did not know I could do is a potent elixir.

Perched on a hill past some farmhouses in the southern tip of Matsuyama City is **Temple 47: Yasakaji (Temple of Eight Slopes)**, so named either because it was carved out of eight slopes or because there are eight paths leading to it. It has a festive look about it, its roof covered with green tiles, and bright, multi-coloured flags adorning its walls.

It has two very interesting features. The first is a dark basement with thousands of statuettes of the Buddhist deity Amida Nyorai, the Buddha of Infinite Light, brought by people from different places. In past travels, I've been to Kamakura, a prominent seaside city just 50 kilometres south-southwest of Tokyo. One of its unforgettable attractions is an impressively large bronze statue of the Great Buddha of Kamakura (Kamakura Daibutsu), in a seated pose, measuring about 13 metres tall and weighing approximately 109 metric tonnes. Only as we are viewing the statuettes of Amida Nyorai in Temple 47 do I learn from Mayumi that the Kamakura Daibutsu is a representation of Amida Nyorai.

The second feature is most unusual and the only one of its kind in the entire pilgrimage – a pair of short tunnels representing the Buddhist heaven and hell. Mayumi decides to explore the tunnel of *jigoku*, or hell. I walk through the tunnel of heaven, or *tengoku*.

'The floor of this tunnel is covered with sharp, pointed stones,' Mayumi calls out. 'The walls have pictures of three evil ways: "the hell way", "the demon's way" and "the animal's way".' She later explains that these represent the realms into which people are reborn, depending on how they behaved when they were alive.

'The floor of the tunnel of heaven is a smooth, pebbled path,' I respond. 'On the wall is a picture of the Pure Land.'

We go through the succeeding temples and end on a high note, with the final one for the day being **Temple 51: Ishiteji (Stone Hand Temple)**. It is a strikingly expansive compound, considered one of the most spectacular on the pilgrimage trail. The entrance gate is classified as a national treasure. The main hall is considered an important cultural property of Japan, along with the bell tower, three-storey pagoda and other halls. An unusual feature is a womb-like cave that connects the inner temple to the main grounds.

AMIDA NYORAI
(Amitabha Tathagata)

●

Amida Nyorai is also known as the Buddha of Infinite Light and the Buddha of Limitless Life. He is the main deity of the Pure Land tradition of Buddhism, where devotees focus on attaining rebirth in the paradise ('Pure Land') presided over by Amida Nyorai. They acquire religious merit through simple meditation and the recitation of prayers or sutras (Buddhist scriptures), with specific mantras and chants to invoke him.

Amida made 48 vows representing his plan to save all sentient beings, the most important of which is the eighteenth, the promise of deliverance. Here, he says, in simple words, that he 'will not abandon anyone'. According to the teaching of the Jodo sect of Buddhism, anyone who recites the name of Amida Buddha will be welcomed into his Pure Land.

Amida Nyorai is often depicted as sitting in a lotus position, with both hands resting on the lap. The back of his right hand is on the palm of the other, with the tips of the thumbs touching one another. This is the mudra of meditation. However, he can be seen too with his hands in one of nine different positions. This is because Amida's Pure Land consists of nine different levels, and devotees believe they will be reborn into one of these.

Amida Nyorai is the main image at **Temples 2, 7, 30, 47, 53, 57, 64, 68** and **78** and one of the five main images at **Temple 37**.

END OF DAY

THERE ARE INNUMERABLE REASONS for making the pilgrimage. I think about the Japanese couple we met today who told us that this was their third time to go on the journey in memory of their departed son. They pray for peace – for him and themselves.

Our paths have crossed at several temples with a man who is making the pilgrimage because he is turning 42 this year. He prays to avert misfortune. The Japanese commonly believe that certain ages are unlucky. There is much regional variation, and different sources specify different ages as dangerous. But it seems broadly accepted that the perilous ages for men are 25, 42 and 61, with 42 being the most inherently dangerous. For women, the calamitous ages are 19, 33 and 37, with 33 being the unluckiest.

It seems to me that, like him, many make this journey in the hope of gaining inner peace, avoiding ill fortune in this lifetime and securing karmic merit for future lifetimes through offerings and prayers in temples.

There is Anika from the Netherlands, who prays for clarity and direction. And the Tibetan monk, who prays for wisdom and guidance as he journeys the path to enlightenment.

Then there is that couple I met a few years back in Koyasan. They shared their story with me as we explored one of the compounds. The husband worked in Tokyo. The wife had been assigned to Tokushima in Shikoku for two years. During those years, when the husband visited his wife in Shikoku, they walked sections of the pilgrimage together. This created a unique constellation of shared experiences, the memories of which helped carry them through each subsequent separation. Their final stop was Koyasan, a joyful thanksgiving after their journey.

So visible in these and other stories are the central themes of love and friendship, pain and loss, exploration and expansion, transition and transcendence. These are the threads that weave the call to adventure into the eternal tapestry that is the pilgrimage. These restless longings have the powerful potential to cast us on the path of awareness, discovery and fulfilment.

We are pilgrims of every denomination, every faith, every belief. But I also sense that genuine oneness is a profound possibility because we all share a common humanity. We each have our own spiritual path, but we honour all others.

Considering the conflicts in the world today, is this aspiration for greater unity of all peoples a lost cause? Once again, the strains of '*Gambatte. Gambatte kudasai*' fill my spirit. 'Please do your best. Don't give up.'

DAY 6

Faith

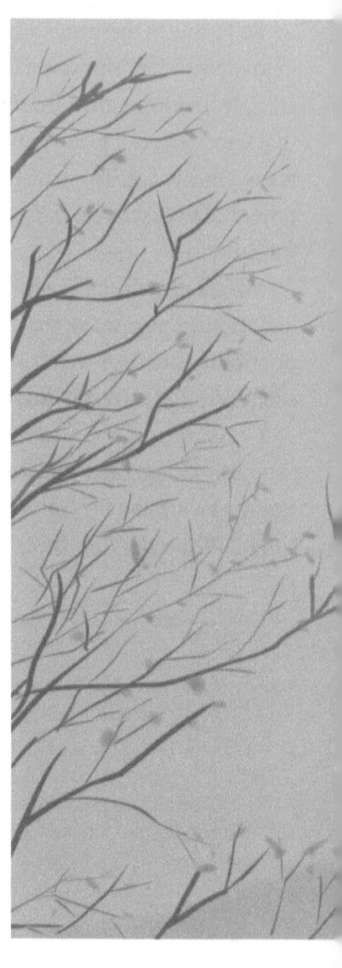

and

Freedom

T
52
—
64

Ehime Prefecture

PASSING THROUGH THE FIRST gate of **Temple 52: Taisanji (Big Mountain Temple)**, I don't realise there's a second gate further up, more impressive than the first, leading to a compound with spectacular views of the Shikoku Mountains.

Ancient folklore tells of how the temple was built overnight by Mano Kogoro, a wealthy merchant who had avoided being shipwrecked through the intervention of Juichimen Kannon. The signage at the temple entrance explains how a storm threatened Mano Kogoro's ship at sea. However, a light emanating from a nearby hill saved him. Washed ashore, he ascended the hill towards the bright light and found a statue of Juichimen Kannon in a small hut. In gratitude, he returned the following day to construct a new temple.

It is still early in the morning, and three *henro* are rousing the sleepy courtyard with their chanting. I stroll over to the incense urn.

I remember not to light my incense stick from the burning sticks already there as that would mean I am taking on the sins of others.

I reach for the second incense stick and then the third. It is customary to offer three sticks of incense, one representing the past, another the present and the third the future. The three sticks also symbolise the so-called *san-mitsu* or body, mouth and mind. The burning of the sticks represents the purification of these.

The reddish glow on the incense stick uncurls and then dances into scented smoke, flicking sparks of tiny stars. Then, as though to lament its decaying ember, a confetti of ash falls sombrely as dark powder. It is a powerful image of transience, the impermanence of nature and life.

All things are in a state of constant change; nothing stays

the same forever. Always becoming, always dying. 'This is the nature of our reality,' I whisper to myself. 'All phenomena and all beings.' Each unfolding experience carries a note of uncertainty.

I think this innate consciousness and acceptance of the fleeting nature of life has birthed an incredible fortitude, resilience and strength of spirit in the Japanese people, which I admire. I have witnessed this repeatedly with my Japanese friends and colleagues.

We make our way to **Temple 53: Enmyoji (Temple of Circular Illumination)**, in a neighbourhood on the outskirts of Matsuyama. Though it is a small compound, the elaborate tiled roofs of the temple buildings are framed elegantly against the cloudless blue of the immense sky, making it appear spacious. A magnificent winged mythical beast is perched intimidatingly on the roof of the *daishido*. Intricately sculpted dragons surround it.

Mayumi says, 'On the lintel of the main hall is a sculpture of a dragon whose eyes flash when it sees a bad person, or so the story goes. The legendary sculptor Hidari Jingoro carved this.'

Later research reveals that Hidari Jingoro is himself a quite intriguing character. Though he is made out to have been a talented carpenter, painter, architect, comedian, actor and professor of art, other accounts

'This too will pass away' is a powerful reminder.
My inner wisdom summons me with urgency
to deeper accountability –
to bring my presence
to the present moment,
lest I squander this precious gift
of possibility and responsibility.

dismiss him as possibly a fictitious Japanese artist. Certainly, controversies abound about his historical existence.

Just off to the side of the temple, as though quietly tucked away, is a small area of graves said to be a 'secret shrine' to the Virgin Mary, venerated in Christianity as the Mother of God.

My curiosity piqued, I approach a vaguely cruciform stone standing on the coarse ground. I am trying to make out precisely what it is when Mayumi translates the signboard for me: 'Christian "cross-shaped" lantern on which a 40-centimetre Maria-Kannon is carved.' The slightly indistinct yet discernible figure carved on the stone is said to be Mary.

'How could this be?' I wonder aloud, as I recall that Christians comprise about one per cent of Japan's population.

In the sixteenth century, a Chinese vessel carrying Portuguese merchants was blown off course and forced to land in Japan. This event paved the way for the first Christian missionaries to introduce Christianity to the islands. The next hundred years marked what came to be known as Japan's 'Christian century'.

However, during the Tokugawa period in the seventeenth century, Christianity was seen as a threat to shogunate power and the social order. Christianity was outlawed. Japanese Christians were tortured and slaughtered. The majority of Europeans were expelled. This was early in Japan's period of isolation, known as *sakoku*, meaning 'closed country' or 'chained country'. Borders were closed to much of the world, except for Chinese traders and a handful of Dutch at Nagasaki. The Christian religion was obliterated from the country, or so it seemed.

I feel a sense of disquiet as I recall the deeply moving yet unsettling film, *Silence*, directed by Martin Scorsese and released in 2016. It is based on the highly acclaimed novel of the same title, written by Shusaku Endo, one of Japan's foremost novelists. Set in Nagasaki in the seventeenth century, it is the story of Portuguese Jesuit missionaries at the height of the persecution of Christians in Japan. Hauntingly beautiful, it plumbs the depths of the human heart that cannot fathom the seeming silence of God in the face of so much suffering. It expresses poignantly how one struggles with the incomprehensible burden of doubt on the path of faith.

These themes certainly dominate much of contemporary reality and sometimes leave me troubled. The movie offers no definitive answers but instead invites us to live the questions beyond the comfortable black-and-white dichotomies of 'right' or 'wrong'. Perhaps this is challenging me to realise that the ultimate truth lies in a realm beyond words.

I feel a kinship with Kichijiro, the deeply flawed, cowardly character in *Silence* who repeatedly betrays God and neighbour and constantly, tearfully, seeks absolution. I am confronted with my countless acts of cowardice, inconstancy and wavering faith. Yet I stumble back to God, again and again, seeking His mercy and grace. It is fitting that in a temple named for the circular nature of illumination, I am thinking about how, at times, my relationship to my own faith can follow a cycle that takes me from certitude to doubt and back to certitude once again.

Standing in this holy site of Enmyoji, I am humbled by the hidden Christians or *kakure kirishitan* who persevered in their faith despite the brutality of the persecution. I touch the cruciform stone and feel a deep admiration for them.

Mayumi explains that it would have been far too risky to sculpt a cross, much less erect it. Instead, by placing a lantern atop the flat surface of the stone, the shape of a cross emerges. This provided a locus for prayer where believers could gather and pay homage to Mary, the Mother of God.

The shogunate wanted to accelerate the extermination of Christianity, so it issued edicts requiring Japanese families to register at the temple nearest them, regardless of whether or not they were believers of Buddhism. Japanese Christians pretended to adopt Buddhist practices while clandestinely putting Christian icons inside Buddhist statues.

Among the plethora of Buddhist statues, the image of Kannon offered the closest resemblance to the Virgin Mary. The origin of Kannon itself as a Buddhist deity is male. But, in the mythical scheme of things, there is also the expression of Kannon in the feminine form, personifying love and inexhaustible compassion.

Buddhist devotees see in this representation the feminine aspect of the Divine. For Japanese Christians, the images of the Buddhist Kannon were a substitute for Mary, the Mother of God, whom they continued to venerate. Maria-Kannon became the name for this combined image of Mother Mary and Kannon. Among the Christians, the occasional depiction of Kannon holding a child was seen as the Virgin Mary and Baby Jesus.[1]

For the hidden Christians, there was a strong similarity between both figures – Kannon and Mary. This resemblance was not only in the external form of a woman holding a child but also in the perceived intrinsic symbolic connection of both being the embodiment of the all-compassionate mother.[2]

I think of this ancient prayer to Mary by an anonymous Christian:

> We take refuge in your mercy, Mother of God. Do not disregard our prayers in troubling times, but deliver us from danger; O only pure one, only blessed one.
>
> *Third to fourth century A.D.*[3]

I experience Mary as more than just an archetype for the divine feminine. In the grace and poetry of Christianity, Mary is exalted in doctrine and dogma as the Mother of Jesus, the incarnate God. And on a purely human level, I can relate personally to her as a woman who walked this earth many centuries ago. I can behold her as my 'Mother', approach her in moments of need and seek her succour and intercession. And I know in my heart that, even before I have asked, she already holds me dearly in her maternal embrace. Because, from my experience as a mother myself, I know that is what mothers do.

'Mayumi,' I say softly, 'do you think the Buddhist monks at this temple knew that Christians were venerating Mary here?'

'Ah,' she replies gently, 'it seems they did. They tolerated this Christian devotion at great risk to their own lives. They were deeply moved by the Christians who persevered in their faith and responded with acceptance and tolerance.'

Temple 53 has been loved by the locals as a kind and beneficent temple. It is one of the few temples, especially in areas of western Japan such as Shikoku and Kyushu, that offer places where Christians can pray.

Then I see a group of Japanese pilgrims paying their respects to Mary at this unassuming shrine. Enveloped in this ambiance of peace and harmony, a deep sense of hope and unity fills my heart. Their reverence touches me.

What, I ask myself, will allow us to be more inclusive of others whose views differ from ours? In this world that has grown so increasingly intolerant of different beliefs and orientations, what is it that keeps us imprisoned in our own points of view? Is fear the real enemy here? Are compassion and forgiveness the keys to genuine understanding?

I tell myself that there is but one divinity that permeates the soul of all humanity, whether we use the name God, Source, Universe, the Infinite Abiding Presence. In the vastness of infinity, is this oneness not sufficient to join all our hearts in a collective embrace of solidarity?

Before proceeding to the next temple, we drive to the nearby Seto Inland Sea, also called Setonaikai, between Japan's main islands of Honshu, Shikoku and Kyushu. We walk towards the calm and tranquil sea and survey its many islands. It is a glorious day, and the place is imbued with a serene atmosphere. How magnificent.

Close to Imabari City is **Temple 54: Enmeiji (Temple of Long Life)**, where Mayumi points out the two separate bell towers in the compound.

'Having two belfries makes this temple unique,' she explains.

Then she recounts an interesting legend.

According to ancient folklore, one of the temple bells was once

I believe in a world that my heart
 knows is possible –
where our human lives are buoyed
by courage and compassion,
by wonderment and wisdom,
lifted and lightened
by humility, heroism and hope;
where Love will endure and prevail.

removed from this site and brought to Matsuyama Castle. Once in Matsuyama Castle, however, the sound made by the bell was like a plea to be brought back home, '*Inuru, inuru*. Home, home.' Consequently, the bell was returned to the original temple.

Other variations of this story say that when thieves attempted to remove the bell, its pealing sound was '*Inuru, inuru*'.

I think to myself that we are all seeking our rightful home. This truth is evident, even in legends.

Temples 54 to 59 are clustered close together. At the centre of Imabari City, we reach **Temple 55: Nankobo (Temple of Southern Lights)**, the only temple on the pilgrimage that honours Daitsu Chisho Nyorai.

DAITSU CHISHO NYORAI
(Mahabhijnajnana-bhibu Buddha)

●

Daitsu Chisho Nyorai, also sometimes referred to as Daitsu Chisho Butsu, is the Buddha of the Past, an ancient Buddha who preceded Shaka Nyorai. While he is relatively unknown, some mythical accounts say there was a distant time when Buddhas like Shaka Nyorai and Amida Nyorai were his followers.

He is often depicted as holding the index finger of his right hand with his left hand (*riken-in*), a hand gesture identified as the 'wisdom fist'.

Daitsu Chisho Nyorai is the main image at **Temple 55**.

I am immediately impressed by its magnificent gate. Housed in the entryway are four fierce temple guards – two in front and two in the back – each intricately carved in wood with gilt highlights.

The lavish entrance hints at the size of the compound, which stretches for three city blocks. The sprawling precinct has temple buildings, shrines and a large and impressive *daishido*.

Interestingly, all but one of the other 88 temples have the typical suffix '*ji*', meaning 'temple', whereas this sacred site is the only one on the route with the suffix '*bo*'. Mayumi says, 'That is so surprising. "Bo" means "small Buddhist temple", but judging by the size of this one, it is probably one of the largest temples we have seen on this pilgrimage.'

I have found myself pleasantly surprised at so many turns on this pilgrimage. Throughout this journey, I continually find myself not just a participant but also an observer of my own thinking and beliefs. And once conscious of them, I can choose whether to continue believing as I do or to believe differently. It is natural to have expectations. But, in my experience, being wedded to these expectations – many of which are self-imposed and arbitrary – leaves little room for surprise and often leads to disappointment and frustration. I have found that if I soften my judgements and am less rigid about my expectations and sharp definitions, I can more easily allow myself to be amazed and discover that I am in the flow of things.

We enter the precinct of **Temple 59: Kokubunji (Official State Temple of Ehime Prefecture)**.

Katsuji laughingly draws me to an unusual feature of this compound. There is a recently sculpted life-size stone statue of Kobo Daishi. He holds a bowl in one hand, and the other hand is outstretched as though inviting one to a handshake.

'You have to make a wish, Yvonne-san,' Katsuji tells me. He demonstrates that he is making his silent wish, and then he reaches out to shake the hand of Kobo Daishi. It is as though Katsuji is literally placing his petition in Kobo Daishi's hands.

I do not have a thought-out wish, but I see that Mayumi is waiting her turn, and I do not want to delay us further. So, with a firm handshake with the statue of Kobo Daishi, I make my wish – joy and peace for both our families.

Then Mayumi reads aloud the sign in Japanese. "It says, 'Only one wish per person'", she translates. "'Please avoid making several wishes because Kobo Daishi is very busy.'"

We all have a good chuckle upon hearing this.

I am wondering, without meaning to split hairs, is joy and peace one wish? Or would that really be two wishes?

As we walk back to the car, I reassure myself that I have made just one wish as I recall a quote I must have read many years ago: 'Joy is peace dancing, and peace is joy at rest.'

Because of the road conditions, we make some adjustment to the order of temples that we will be visiting. So from Temple 59 we proceed to Temple 61 through to Temple 64, ending the day with a visit to Temple 60.

Most temples on the route have a countryside or mountainside feel, hemmed in by trees, overgrown grass, or foothills. **Temple 61: Koonji (Incense Garden Temple)** stands close to the foothills of Mount Ishizuchi in Saijo. I was expecting it to have that countryside feel again, seeing its beautiful surroundings in verdant shades.

Imagine then my surprise as I come upon an enormous building of poured concrete, drab and grey. I am not attracted to it as I prefer the graceful curves of arches on wooden temples, multi-storey pagodas, or a backdrop of cascading waterfalls, as we have seen in previous temples. I enter the main hall anyway, although it reminds me of a lecture theatre or college auditorium. I am glad I do so, however, for inside stands a splendid golden statue of Dainichi Nyorai, a principal deity in Buddhism.

The dangling bells, candles and electric lanterns draw attention to this most eminent Buddha in his classic pose. The five fingers of the right hand embrace the index finger of his left, a distinctive gesture associated with this deity.

'Mayumi,' I call out, 'I read somewhere that this particular gesture symbolises the unity of the five worldly elements – earth, water, fire, air or wind and space or void – with spiritual consciousness. Am I right?'

Mayumi nods approvingly, as a teacher might with a student who has just given the correct answer.

It so happens that I had heard about Jin Shin Jyutsu (JSJ), a modality of Japanese energetic healing, even before moving to Japan. A doctor at a health resort in the Philippines introduced this natural healing mode to me. I was immediately intrigued by the doctor's success stories with her patients. At the risk of oversimplifying things, JSJ says that a primary emotion or attitude is associated with each finger, and that holding that finger helps harmonise that emotion. Interestingly, fear is related to the index finger. In some way, all negative emotions are a variant of fear.[4]

DAINICHI NYORAI
(Vairocana; Mahavairocana)

Dainichi Nyorai is the Great Buddha of Universal Illumination, sometimes called the Cosmic Buddha. In Japanese Esoteric Buddhism, Dainichi Nyorai is the most eminent of all the different Buddhas. Hence, he is the main object of veneration, often supplanting the historical Buddha. He is also the central figure in the Shingon mandala (visual representation of the Buddhist world), scrolls and paintings. Shingon Buddhism asserts that human beings also have the Buddha nature and the life force of Dainichi Nyorai.

Dainichi Nyorai is portrayed as a seated figure, best recognised by his most distinctive hand gesture. The digits of the right hand, symbolising the five elements of the material realm, clasp the index finger of the left hand (*chiken-in*), representing the Buddhist essence of the spiritual realm. This hand position is called the 'wisdom fist' or the 'knowledge fist' mudra. It represents the union of the material and the spiritual realms and speaks to the power to restrain passions that might hinder enlightenment.

Unlike other Buddhas, Dainichi Nyorai is typically depicted with luxurious adornments and accessories such as a crown on his head and a string of beads or lacework on his neck, chest, arms, wrists and legs. Another clear identifier is a double halo, one for the head and another for the body, symbolising the light emitted by the Buddha.

Dainichi Nyorai is the central object of reverence at **Temples 4, 28, 42, 60, 61** and **72**.

I believe that we can choose to live in love or fear, the latter often being a belief in lack or limitation. I am reminded to harmonise my fears so that I may be liberated to make a conscious choice to live in love, which calls us to be more trusting in life.

It is early afternoon, and we find ourselves in **Temple 63: Kichijoji (Temple of Mahasri or Laksmi)**. This temple is unique because it is the only one on the Shikoku pilgrimage route with Bishamonten as its main image. The temple seems to be named in honour of Kichijoten, the wife of Bishamonten, whose statue also stands on the temple grounds. It is said that Kobo Daishi carved both of these statues.

> **BISHAMONTEN (VAISRAVANA)**
>
> ●
>
> Bishamonten, sometimes called Bishamon, is the god of war and punisher of evil. He is the guardian of Buddhist temples and places where Buddha is teaching. He is often portrayed as well versed in the teachings of Buddha. He is also usually found guarding Buddha (in statue form) himself. He is considered the Lord of Wealth and Treasure, for which reason he is included in the group of Seven Lucky Gods for people wishing for good fortune.
>
> As the god of war, he is usually depicted as being armed with a sword in his right hand. As well, his left hand holds a pagoda that is said to house the Buddha's ashes.
>
> Bishamonten is the primary image at **Temple 63**.

A small rock with a hole in the middle is of interest in the temple complex. It is said that the gods will grant your wish if you can walk towards the stone with your eyes closed and successfully stick your staff into the hole. Mayumi and I have no such luck, but attempting this has given us a great laugh, so we leave in a light-hearted mood.

The end of the day finds us at **Temple 60: Yokomineji (Side Summit or Peak Temple)**. Once again, I am grateful that we are making the trip by car as this is another one of those temples notorious with the walking *henro* for its steep and challenging trails. It is said to be the most *nansho* or difficult to reach temple of all *nansho*.

Our spirits are high as we make the winding drive up the thickly forested mountain to the car park. Then we walk the wooded trail to the temple grounds at 709 metres above sea level, the third highest on the route.

I have my *kongozue* with me as I stroll in awe across the expansive compound and through its vast, meticulously tended garden featuring rhododendrons and hydrangeas, multiple paths and wooden Buddhist sculptures. I see all this beauty and cannot help but feel that this is the generous reward for all our persistence and efforts to reach this temple.

It is the perfect note on which to end the day. After almost an hour's drive to our hotel, we refresh ourselves with a delightful meal of fresh sashimi (raw fish), and then we turn in for the night.

END OF DAY

I QUICKLY SCAN MY memories of Day 6. I am reminded again of a simplicity that touches me deeply about this pilgrimage journey. It is not so much that our lodgings are spartan and unpretentious. Nor even that most of our meals comprise simple fare purchased from roadside convenience stores. Nor that we carry in our backpacks only the most unassuming basics of a travel wardrobe. Nor even that we have limited or no access to television and the internet.

Instead, it is the simplicity of warm hospitality in the places that we have visited. It is the simplicity of a trusting heart whose sighs speak power in the silence. It is the simplicity of a stranger's warm smile, a kind offering of food or drink, or, when ascending a challenging trail, the heartfelt, encouraging words from fellow pilgrims.

Excess in any form can be a distraction and the simplicity I am experiencing on this trip somehow deepens my appreciation of the value of life and how we can care for and interact with others.

THOUGHTS

DAY 7

Rendezvous

and

Redemption

65
Ehime Prefecture

66
|
79
Kagawa Prefecture

THE FOURTEENTH-CENTURY MYSTICAL PERSIAN poet Hafiz said, 'I am happy even before I have a reason.' That is how I feel today, Day 7 of our pilgrimage.

We are moving towards the north-eastern part of Shikoku, and today we intend to visit ten temples. The plan is to travel to three prefectures in the first hours of the day. We will start the day with a visit to Temple 65, the last temple in Ehime Prefecture. Then we will proceed towards Kagawa Prefecture, the smallest in Japan, which accounts for only about 0.5 per cent of the total land area of the entire country. Temple 66 is almost on the border between Kagawa Prefecture and Tokushima Prefecture, the latter being where we started our pilgrimage seven days ago. From there, we will head to the rest of the temples in Kagawa Prefecture. According to Buddhist tradition, Temples 66 to 88 correspond to the spiritual topography of the Dojo of Nirvana.

Our first stop for the day, **Temple 65: Sankakuji (Triangle Temple)**, is the last sacred site in the Dojo of Enlightenment. Its name goes back to the story about Kobo Daishi building a triangular altar at which he performed a prayer ritual to expel a ghost causing trouble in the area. There is also a small triangular island in the pond where the altar once stood.

It is an impressive temple set into the mountains and worth every one of the countless ancient, worn stone steps that I have to climb to reach it. Splendid wooden carvings adorn the different buildings in the peaceful compound, which is enveloped in calm. The quietness of the morning is interrupted in the most subtle of ways only by a distant birdsong.

I feel the warm sun on my face, though the dew still lingers on the grass like delicate glass beads, prisms of the morning light. Content and serene, I stand with my eyes closed and my arms outstretched to the deep clear blue of the sky. It is a somewhat strange experience, but within me I get the sense of the vastness of God in the stillness. With the breeze brushing against my cheeks, I feel His embrace in the gentlest, most tender of ways.

I breathe in deeply the fresh morning air and feel the joy of simply being alive. Alive and blessed. How wonderful is that. A sense of abundance enfolds me. There is the generous warmth of the sun. Cotton-like clouds float across the vast blue sky. The glistening blades of grass shimmer in the early morn.

I take into my heart the blessing of this new day, my simple prayer nurturing both body and spirit.

What a perfect way, I say to myself, to be ushered into the next set of temples in the Dojo of Nirvana. These hallowed grounds with nary a ripple of disturbance are, metaphorically, paving our transition to the next temples representing peace and happiness on this sacred journey.

We use the ropeway to bring us to **Temple 66: Unpenji (Hovering Clouds Temple)**. It is a fitting name. Standing at 911 metres above sea level, it is the highest mountain temple of the entire Shikoku pilgrimage. Unpenji is listed as a temple of Kagawa Prefecture, but, strangely enough, it is actually on the prefectural border in Tokushima. Nevertheless, we are at an exciting juncture in our pilgrimage. We have entered the last prefecture, Kagawa, known in ancient times as Sanuki. It is the birthplace of Kobo Daishi.

In the cable-car ride of a mere seven minutes, the experience reveals the incredible gift of perspective. On one level, I see how the countryside spreads out and how the buildings, the cars and the people gradually shrink, while the trees dwindle gracefully into the distance. On another level, my preoccupations recede, small and insignificant, in the bigger picture of a life lived meaningfully, purposefully and joyfully.

As we make our way from the cable-car station to the main temple buildings, we are greeted by hundreds of life-sized stone statues called arhats or *rakan* (worthy ones).

'These are the 500 disciples of Buddha who have gained insight into the true nature of existence,' Mayumi says. 'By meditation and rigorous spiritual practice, they have attained nirvana. Many temples have *rakan*, but the ones here are full-sized, so they look real.'

'Look,' Katsuji adds. 'Each statue exhibits a different facial expression.'

These *rakan*, disciples of Buddha, achieved the ultimate goal of all Buddhists: nirvana – liberation from the endless cycle of rebirth and the extinction of attachment, hatred and ignorance. They followed the path of the Buddha, Shaka Nyorai (Siddhartha Gautama).

They remind me of the Christian saints who passed from the pain, the suffering and the transience of this worldly life into eternal happiness with God in heaven through faith in Jesus Christ.

At the exact moment that I am thinking about this, my attention is drawn to a small courtyard. Past a row of *rakan* statues is a prominent seven-tiered pagoda, in front of which is a sculpture depicting the historical Buddha. He is lying on his right side in the sleep of death, his pillow aligned to the north. As he enters paranirvana, otherwise known as nirvana-after-death, he is surrounded by disciples and other personages who witness his passing and are mourning.

Walking a bit further, we encounter a fascinating fixture that looks like a hollow portal in the shape of an eggplant (aubergine) on a stone slab. As I stand there trying to decipher what it is, Mayumi comes yet again to the rescue, eagerly instructing me to walk through the opening in the centre or to go around and sit on the colossal eggplant sculpture on the other side.

'Then make a wish,' she says. She has read about these sculptures in some Japanese texts on the pilgrimage.

Seeing that I do not quite get the connection, Mayumi patiently explains to me, 'The Japanese word for eggplant, *nasu*, is a homonym for "to achieve" or "to attain".' She shares a bit of trivia with me. 'Do you know that every eggplant flower becomes an eggplant?'

'That is so interesting,' I respond. 'I did not know that at all.'

Oddly, a curious wish emerges from somewhere within me, so peculiar that even I am intrigued. But I have learned to trust inner wisdom in unexpected moments like this. So I make my wish. In my mind's eye, I imagine that I am opening the 'spiritual backpack' I am lugging around on my journey – my physical, emotional, psychological and spiritual journey. And I am removing from it the pebbles, the stones, the rocks – and all that they represent – that are weighing me down. If I just let them go, how much lighter will I feel? How much faster can I go?

If I could, I would toss away the countless pebbles of toxic old habits and vain, egotistical strivings. I would throw away the rocks of stale, self-limiting beliefs, malleable bars in the prison of my own making. I would cast away the accumulated stones of persistent worries, fears, anger, sorrows and energy-draining moments when I try to be someone other than who I really am.

According to Buddhism, the enlightened mind is unshackled by negative mental states and emotions such as doubt, fear and anxiety. Nirvana is the state of perfect quietude, complete and everlasting peace.

I, too, seek to be free from all that weighs down my spirit. I, too, want to know the splendour of the glorious kingdom of light and peace. What speaks most to my heart at this moment is the powerful observation made by St Augustine more than 1,600 years ago: 'You have made us for yourself, O Lord, and our hearts are restless until they rest in you.'

Notwithstanding our differences in beliefs, Katsuji, Mayumi and I share a common conviction that something much more profound is possible beyond the wild anxieties, the vexing problems, the empty vanities that bind and burden us in this life. Somehow, we cling to the hope – each in our own way – that beyond this earthly reality is a place, a state of unbounded peace, unfathomable compassion and unparalleled joy.

It is still early morning. The quietness of this hour induces introspection in my meditative wander around the temple complex, even as Mayumi and Katsuji go off exploring some side paths. My heart is soaring, and on this graceful summit I feel as though I can walk the clouds.

We gather at the designated meeting place at the agreed time to take the ropeway back to the main road. The descent from Temple 66 reveals the staggeringly beautiful vistas of the surrounding Chugoku region and the Seto Inland Sea.

Perhaps
all our different faiths
are but the rays
of the same Eternal Sun.
It is
ONE divine Light
that shines forth in us.

So much incredible beauty exists in our world right now. Imagine how much more beautiful would be the wondrous realm we desire beyond this life. That state of everlasting peace and joy would be much more gratifying than our best aspirations and more deeply fulfilling than all our fondest hopes and dreams.

There is an air of joviality in the car on our way to **Temple 67: Daikoji (Temple of the Great Growth)**, a majestic temple located in a grove.

Suddenly, Mayumi exclaims, 'Oh, we are so lucky. That's the chief priest.' She points to a man in gold and navy robes walking about the grounds. The mood builds to a palpable excitement.

We eagerly approach him, and he is immediately warm and welcoming. Mayumi tells him in Japanese that I have come from Australia to make the pilgrimage. His broad smile conveys delight that I have come a long way and am now visiting this temple.

Through Mayumi, he asks me how I am finding the pilgrimage so far. I reply that the journey has been full of wonderful discoveries, experiences and insights. I add that I am learning so many things.

He nods and says in Japanese, 'There is always much to learn if one has an open heart.'

Yes, indeed. In Japan, there are moments when I would like to get into a deeper conversation but am unable to do so because I don't speak Japanese and the other party does not speak English. This encounter is one of those moments.

We walk a few paces in silence. It is not an uncomfortable quietude. In Japan, I have found that people tend to be more comfortable with silence, even for long durations, than in the West. My experience in Japan, interacting with Japanese people, has led me to perceive that they have an uncanny ability to 'read the atmosphere', so to speak, to listen for what is felt but not said. I have learned to be comfortable with this kind of silence and tap into inner sensitivity that enables me to grasp what is spoken and what is not.

Though only a few words are exchanged, mutual respect is expressed. Kind wishes, though unspoken, are conveyed and acknowledged. To use a Christian phrase, a shared ministry of presence affirms our connection in the great web of relationships across all of life.

Emerging full-hearted from this encounter, I cannot wait to visit the rest of the temples in this Dojo of Nirvana that takes us to the 'end' of the pilgrimage.

The Japanese nutmeg and camphor trees, with their brilliant green leaves seen against the grey sky, add a vibrant atmosphere to the open grounds of Temple 67. A spicy, aromatic, woody scent fills the air.

I have seen so often
how compassion, courage
  and consideration
create a stream of goodness
  and generosity
that ripples rivers of peace
  throughout the world.
In my heart, I know
it matters not who or what one is –
simply that we are all
  interconnected
in this one web of life.

A Japanese woman wearing a long white apron and rubber sandals is in the compound, just a few metres from me. She turns in my direction, and our eyes meet long enough for me to catch the smile radiating from hers. She shuffles over to me, her sandals gently slapping the stone slabs.

She bows gracefully. '*Ohenro san*. Honourable pilgrim. *Osettai*. A gift,' she explains, holding out a cup of tea to me.

I bow awkwardly and then stretch out my hands to receive the small ceramic container. '*Arigato gozaimasu*, thank you very much,' I say, bowing again to express my deep appreciation.

'Good Japanese. Good Japanese.' She beams with much delight and encouragement. It is a typical reaction to a foreigner's attempt to say just a few words in the local language. Gleefully, she invites me to approach a table where other Japanese women in long white aprons or loose white blouses are standing. With extraordinary graciousness, they greet me with warm smiles and pour me more tea. I feel immensely welcome.

One of them quickly offers a *dorayaki*, a small pancake with a red-bean filling. Another reaches for a little crocheted ornament to give me. The woman standing closest to me eagerly asks from which country I come. She is visibly happy on this occasion to practise her rudimentary English. An impressed murmur escapes her lips when I tell her I come from Australia. We proceed to make some small talk.

'*Osettai, osettai*. A gift, a gift,' they tell me as they offer me more sweets.

Taking a bite, I exclaim, '*Oishi*. Delicious.' They giggle shyly.

At the beginning of the pilgrimage, I thought that giving material gifts or services was simply a basic expression of support to ease a burden or encourage a pilgrim on a journey. Now, I know this is how the offeror of *osettai* participates in the pilgrimage. The pilgrim is, in some sense, an intermediary that affords the giver vicarious participation in the journey. It is a beautiful sentiment.

I now understand in a more profound way that while the pilgrim is the recipient of kindness, the gesture is directed towards Kobo Daishi, in whose footsteps the pilgrim follows. *Dogyo ninin* – 'we are two travelling in company'.

Energised by this encounter, I leave the temple grounds with renewed enthusiasm and determination. What the gift is and what the giver receives in return are of no consequence. The intangible spirit of reciprocity lies at the heart of this human interaction. One human being connects to another in an exchange of the true gift graciously offered and gratefully received. It is a celebration of humanity, regardless of age, race, gender or religion.

It is early afternoon. News is being broadcast in Japanese on the car radio. I can tell there is some excitement in the air from the lively voices of Mayumi and Katsuji, who are in animated conversation.

While unable to understand the announcement, I surmise that it is about the recent crowning of Prince Naruhito as the 126th emperor of the Japanese monarchy, the world's oldest continuous hereditary dynasty. Because of old age and declining health, 85-year-old Emperor Akihito abdicated the throne to his elder son, Crown Prince Naruhito, four days ago, on the first of May 2019. On that occasion, the 31-year-long Heisei era of the former ended, and the latter's new imperial era, called Reiwa, began.

Japan is the only country globally that uses the era system called *gengo*. Japan's first recorded imperial era was in the year 645 C.E. and was named the Taika era, under Emperor

Kotoku. But it was not until the Meiji Restoration, the political revolution of 1868, that the practice of assigning an era name for the entire duration of an emperor's reign began. Before that, the *gengo* could change for various reasons, such as a national disaster or an epidemic.

The Reiwa era is the fifth imperial age of the last century and a half, following the four other eras: Meiji (1868–1912), Taisho (1912–1926), Showa (1926–1989) and Heisei (1989–2019). The imperial era identifies the years on the Japanese calendar corresponding to the emperor's reign and is used on state documents, newspapers, calendars, driving licences and currency.

I smile as I recall how I first felt confused at filling in 'Heisei era' alongside the Western Gregorian calendar dates on different official documents relating to my Tokyo assignment in the past years.

And now, at the beginning of the new imperial age, I feel thrilled as I am looking at a separate vermilion stamp that we have received in **Temple 74: Koyamaji (Armour Mountain Temple)**.

The red circle in the centre of the page says 'Shikoku 88 Koyamaji the 74th'. The stamp's design is a rabbit, making me recall the rabbit statues on the temple roof and in the temple grounds. The temple store even offered rabbit-shaped lucky charms and sweets.

But what delights me are the black kanji on the right-hand side, which say, '5 May, First Year of Reiwa'. For me, having the date written on this stamp makes it truly special, given that we are in precisely the very first days of this new era.

We have indeed had our *nokyocho* imprinted with the red pilgrim's stamp in all the temples we have visited on this Shikoku circuit. The stamps identify the name of the temple and indicate the principal deity. However, the date of the visit is not written, unlike in other temples outside this pilgrimage route.

There is a reason for this. A *henro* who makes the pilgrimage again at another time simply presents the same *nokyocho* to the temple scribe to get it stamped. Since no date is indicated on the stamped page, it can be used repeatedly, however often a *henro* makes the pilgrimage. The red stamp indicating the temple name is imprinted on the *nokyocho* as many times as the pilgrim visits that temple.

This being a new era, however, I feel the moment has some historical significance, and I am delighted to have a separate stamped sheet with today's date in Japanese – '5 May, First Year of Reiwa'!

As I hold the red seal from Koyamaji, I cannot help feeling that I am in some subtle way participating in a momentous occasion. The historic abdication of Emperor Akihito is Japan's first in more than two centuries. And the *gengo* term 'Reiwa' is also, in some way, a break with tradition. Whereas past imperial era names were derived from classical Chinese literature, 'Reiwa' was taken from the *Manyoshu*, the oldest collection of Japanese poems.

In addition, a new era name is significant in that it sets the tone for the coming decades. The Meiji era meant 'Enlightened Rule' in English. The Taisho era meant 'Great Righteousness'. The Showa era was translated as 'Enlightened Harmony' and the Heisei era stood for 'Achieving Peace'. And now, this new Reiwa era has been translated as 'Beautiful Harmony'.

I fervently wish that this new imperial age signals fresh hope for the Japanese people.

Stories are the fabric of any pilgrimage, and the many legends that abound in Shikoku are the bedrock of its route, rhythm and cherished rituals. Arriving at **Temple 77: Doryuji (Temple of Arising Way)**, I rediscover a story whose significance I only now understand, even though I've heard it before.

The story goes back more than 1,200 years. Indeed, we now know of the great Buddhist priest Kobo Daishi, the main protagonist of the sacred stories of Shikoku. We know that he was born in Shikoku, walked this land of mountains, sky and sea and, through his deeds of wonder, brought hope for enlightenment in this lifetime to many followers.

But then there is the story of Emon Saburo, a key antagonist in the drama that unfolded in ancient times.[1] His legacy helped spell the beginnings of the route, rhythm and ritual of the Shikoku pilgrimage through a matrix of interrelated tales and stories.

In the ninth century, there lived a man of opulence and power who was greedy and hard-hearted. That man was Emon Saburo, and the place was Ebara in Iyo Province, now known as Ehime Prefecture.

One day, a lowly wandering pilgrim came to Saburo's house, held out his begging bowl and pleaded for some food. But he was coldly turned away. The next day, the same mendicant monk appeared again at Saburo's doorway. But the response to his humble pleas was abhorrent – human excrement dumped in his bowl, and cruel rejection.

The monk returned the next day and the next, each time rebuffed. Finally, in a fit of anger on the eighth day, the contemptuous Saburo took a stick and hit the monk's begging bowl, causing it to shatter into eight pieces.

The number eight has been widely recognised as the symbol of infinity. In Buddhism, the number eight comes up over and over again. The Eightfold Path, a ramification of the Buddha's principal teaching of the Four Noble Truths. The Eight Great Bodhisattvas who embody the Eightfold Path. The Eighth Stage or *bhumi*, the irreversible state of enlightenment. The Eight Auspicious Symbols, including the Eight Spokes of the Wheel that symbolise the Buddha's teaching. The commemoration of Buddha's enlightenment on the eighth of December. Then, of course, there are the eight mountains surrounding Mount Koya.

And, in this story of Emon Saburo, the monk's begging bowl splintered into eight fragments.

At that, the monk left and returned no more.

The day after this incident, Saburo's eldest son died. On the following day, another child died. And so it was that Saburo's children died one by one over the next few days. By the eighth day, Saburo had lost every one of his eight children.

Overcome with unbearable grief, Saburo was drowning in heartache. One night, the monk appeared to him in a dream, making him see the error of his ways. Saburo then realised that the monk he had repeatedly turned away so vehemently was Kobo Daishi.

The repentant Saburo left home in search of the monk, to ask his forgiveness. He set out on a pilgrim's path, circling the island of Shikoku in a clockwise fashion for four years. With a sedge hat on his head, a walking stick in one hand and a begging bowl in the other, he became like the monk who had come to his home, pleading for alms. But Saburo could not catch up with Kobo Daishi, who seemed to be always just a few steps ahead of him.

After his twentieth time circling the island, Saburo concluded that if the monk was going clockwise, he, Saburo, would have a better chance of meeting him if he went anticlockwise. He started to walk in the opposite direction, but the journey had by now begun to take its toll on him. Just as he felt his life was slipping away, Saburo encountered Kobo Daishi in the mountains near Temple 12 and begged his forgiveness. Kobo Daishi forgave him, comforted him in his last moments and asked for his dying wish.

Saburo's final wish was to be reborn as the ruler of Iyo Province so that he could use the power of that position to do good and to right the wrongs he had done in his life. Kobo Daishi picked up a small stone, wrote on it and pressed it into the left hand of Saburo as he breathed his last.

Legend has it that a baby boy was born to an influential feudal lord of Yuzuki Castle in Matsuyama, Ehime Prefecture, several centuries later. The child's fist was closed from birth, as though tightly clutching something. When the child was three years old, the chief priest of Annyuji (the former name of Temple 51) was called in to chant special invocations to enable the child to open his hand. The child's hand relaxed to reveal a small stone on which was written 'Emon Saburo reborn'.

The child grew up to be a wise ruler of Yuzuki Castle, and Annyuji Temple was renamed Ishiteji, meaning Stone Hand Temple.

The guidebook says that the egg-shaped stone said to bear the message of Emon Saburo's reincarnation is found in Temple 51, although it is too big to fit in the tiny hand of a newborn baby. I did not notice the stone when we were in that temple as it is one of the busier temples on the route, with its souvenir stalls, tour groups and a kaleidoscope of religious imagery. Neither was I aware of the area near Temple 46 where the burial mounds of Saburo's children are said to be located.

Almost all the signs on the pilgrimage route and in the temple compounds are in Japanese, so I miss things simply by not knowing the language. A great example of this was when we arrived at one temple and, on seeing a Japanese sign with a red arrow pointing to the left, I naturally started off in that direction.

Mayumi called out to me, 'Yvonne-san, Yvonne-san, where are you going?'

'I'm following the red arrow,' I said. 'Isn't it pointing to the main hall?'

Quite bemused, she said, 'The sign says "Toilet". Is that where you want to go?'

I laughingly retraced my steps to join Mayumi on the path towards the right side, where the main hall was located.

Still, this experience is likely a metaphor for life. In my life, there are many things, gifts and miracles I overlook too when I am engulfed in busyness and don't pay attention or am simply not attuned to the silent promptings of the Spirit or to consciousness expressing itself in the present moment. I become aware of all this when I sit in stillness each day, even if only for a few minutes.

I feel that, being often immersed in the routine of habitual expectations, we may miss profound truths in our inner or outer worlds. Or we may assume, often unwittingly, that the world is a certain way. As diarist Anaïs Nin tells us, 'We see the world not as it is but as we are.'

Somehow, a message we perhaps missed earlier may resurface later to catch our attention. This is how I have experienced the universe at work sometimes too.

And so, on this trip, it is at Temple 77, where I see the statue of Emon Saburo kneeling in repentance before Kobo Daishi, that I begin to read more intently about this legend. On his head sits a red cap, similar to the handmade hats presented to Jizos in order to obtain karmic merit.

Indeed, I think, Emon Saburo must have been the first lay pilgrim – or at least among the very first – who followed in the footsteps of the priest Kobo Daishi. Did the clockwise direction of his travels set the traditional circuit for the pilgrimage? When he set out in the opposite direction, was that presenting an alternative route to future pilgrims?

On his twenty-first turn around the island, Saburo finally encountered the monk he was seeking. Might this have set the rhythm for pilgrims to make the pilgrimage multiple times? We met a Japanese couple who had walked the route three times, and we've heard stories of pilgrims who have made the pilgrimage more than ten times or even 20 times.

The structure of the pilgrimage as a circular trail facilitates a recurrent process. On a linear route, the pilgrim gets to the defined end point. The next logical step is to return home through the standard means of transportation. Many pilgrims can experience this as an unpleasant disruption of the rhythm or focus they have built during the pilgrimage.[2]

However, with the Shikoku pilgrimage, although the pilgrim may have reached the final temple in their journey, they may simply carry on, since they are still on the same circular route. From various accounts, some pilgrims become practically permanent fixtures on the Shikoku *henro* as they complete the pilgrimage repeatedly. Motivations differ from one pilgrim to the next, just as they differ from one pilgrimage to the next, even for the same pilgrim. Every round is an opportunity to engage with life in a new way. And every time they return, there is a newness in the air, the promise of fresh beginnings, perhaps a more profound transformation. So, what may have started as the pilgrimage of a lifetime could morph into a lifetime of pilgrimage.[3]

And there are elements of pilgrimage rituals that one can glean from the legend of Emon Saburo. It is said, for instance, that at the sacred sites he visited he left name slips that were the precursor of those now used. In those days, pilgrims wrote their names on pieces of wood called *osamefuda*. They then nailed these to the walls of the temples. This was Saburo's way of letting Kobo Daishi know he was chasing him.

My experience of the warm hospitality with which locals have welcomed me, this practice of *osettai*, probably has its roots in the belief that any pilgrim could be Kobo Daishi in disguise. Learning the lessons from the legend of Emon Saburo, one would not want to mistreat even the lowliest pilgrim.

Beyond route, rhythm and ritual, however, what I learn from the legend of Emon Saburo are lessons in renewal, rendezvous and redemption. We make journeys – inner and outer – where we seek inward reformations or transformations. For many, perhaps the pilgrimage is one such journey of renewal. The rendezvous is not so much about the people and experiences we encounter on this journey. Instead, it is about the better versions of ourselves that emerge in the course of our wandering. And redemption? Ah. That is when we find ourselves restored to a higher sense of purpose.

> It is said,
> 'You are the author of your life story.'
> This being so, then I am free to rewrite it.
> I am not limited by what I have done,
> where I have gone, who I have been.
> Calling on grace, wisdom and truth,
> I can take radical responsibility
> for who I am willing to be –
> that is only a conscious choice away.

END OF DAY

BACK IN THE HOTEL, it is only as I review the day that I notice a paragraph in my guidebook that I overlooked earlier. It points to the origin story of **Temple 73: Shusshakaji (Temple of Shaka Nyorai's Appearance)**, of which many versions exist.[4]

Set in the rugged, wooded mountains, the legend describes how, at age seven, Kobo Daishi walked unhesitatingly to a precarious cliff.

He called out to the Buddha and boldly vowed that he would save many people by devoting his life to the relentless pursuit of Buddhahood. He felt he did not deserve to live if he could not fulfil this vow. With those determined words, he threw himself over the cliff's edge, his hands pressed together in prayer.

At that instant, the child plummeting downwards from the precipice was caught in the embrace of the Buddha. Some accounts say angels caught him. And in the next magical moment, Kobo Daishi the child was carried to safety, destined for a life of eternal service to the Dharma, the doctrine of Buddha.

How, I marvel, did Kobo Daishi even know what he wanted to do with his life at that tender age of seven? My mind harks back to a memory from decades ago of an endearing moment with my son, John, the younger of my two boys, who, until then, had only ever been in an all-boys' primary school. He asked me with the pure innocence of a very young child, 'Mama, when you were a little boy, what did you want to be when you grew up?'

The story of Kobo Daishi confronts me with the questions: Who am I? What is it that truly matters to me? What am I willing to die for? Or, maybe more importantly, what is it that I am living for or think I am living for?

Then it strikes me that these are the questions Jesus asks. To the blind man, he says, 'What do you want?' The blind man responds, 'I want to see.'

The first recorded question Jesus asks of his disciples is 'What are you looking for?' They sidestep the question by asking, 'Where are you staying?' Perhaps they don't know what they truly are looking for. Or perhaps they want to know a bit more about who he is, where he lives and what kind of person he might be. His answer is at once annoying and elusive, even as it is undeniably concrete: 'Come and see.'

This is the invitation to walk the path that leads to him – perhaps one that will make the difference in our never-ending quest for purpose and meaning, happiness and freedom. This is the invitation to discipleship, the path of life's pilgrimage. Is this, I wonder, meant to be my heart's journeying until I reach my eternal home?

I feel he is asking these questions of me now, as I know he will ask me again and again at various moments of my life. 'What are you looking for? What do you want?'

I answer as the blind man does. 'I want to see.'

DAY 8

Completion

and

Celebration

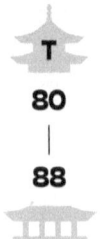

T
80
—
88

Kagawa Prefecture

SITTING QUIETLY IN THE dawn hours, I reminisce about the paths we have traversed over the past seven days.

There are paths that are abandoned, paths that beckon, paths that unexpectedly bring a change to the horizon. There are paths that produce itineraries, confuse directionalities and form linkages or dichotomies. So many paths seem to be etched in nature and embossed on the land, shaping and defining the external landscape waiting to be explored.

They are an excellent metaphor for our inner journeys, the paths we meander in search of meaning and purpose, success and significance, impact and contribution.

Whether walking the entire pilgrimage or going by some means of transportation, paths reveal themselves, particularly in the approach to the temples. Some car parks are located almost directly in front of the temple gate or are just a quick, pleasant stroll away, over sometimes level, albeit uneven, terrain. Without a doubt, these have been the easiest for me to navigate. Even so, the temple grounds always hold a sense of suspense somehow.

What at first seemed like a small temple precinct has often opened up to reveal steep stone steps, trails among towering cedars, winding walkways weaving through hidden statues or even maze-like corridors in dark, confined spaces. And what unexpected treasures to be discovered along the paths. Like a stroll through flower fields or amid wisteria vines.

For other temples, the car parks are located some distance from the temple gate, requiring a fair bit of walking to get to the entrance. Again, I have been intrigued by the variety of paths and temple approaches, not to mention the memorable experiences encountered on many of them.

There are paths that braid through latticed roots, cling to uneven rocks, trace rivers, scale ridges and cut across ravines. There are paths that lie straight, paths that snake through the forest, paths that ascend mountains to reveal ethereal views draped in mist.

There are temples easily accessed from the main road, located at a busy street intersection. Other temples are atop several flights of stone steps. Still others are reached only after a steep climb along undulating terrain.

Some paths cross landscaped gardens; others follow sloped forests. Others are part of cultural traditions, where you climb a certain number of steps, taking care to leave a few coins on these steps in order to exorcise bad karma relating especially to the unlucky ages for men and women.

Then there are ropeways that transport pilgrims to temples in mountains mysteriously imbued with history and culture. Riding high above cedar forests and small towns has been breathtaking, the mountains rising around us then reluctantly retreating into the thickening mist, the cables of the ropeway triumphantly dominating the view outside the gondola.

We will encounter more paths today, so I take a few minutes to enter into a quiet reflection before heading out. In this state of present-moment mindfulness, I remind myself to choose with grace and wisdom the inner paths I decide to traverse. The thoughts I harbour carve my patterns of thinking and mindset. The emotions I revisit shape the deep landscape of my heart. If I stay only in the entangled familiar, I shackle my curiosity. And if I forget how to laugh, I may lose the magic of a moment.

> Walking my inner and outer path
> is more a matter of becoming
> rather than simply doing.

We set out for the prefectural temple of Kagawa, **Temple 80: Kokubunji (Official State Temple of Kagawa Prefecture)**, the first destination in our day's itinerary. Just past its entrance gate is a beautiful promenade lined on both sides with 88 stone statues, miniature replicas of the main images enshrined in the temples of the Shikoku *henro*. The *daishido* also functions as a temple shop, and Mayumi buys a simple black canvas tote – the number 88 is written in big white letters, below which is the line: 'Life is *HENRO*'.

There are no stores, restaurants or vending machines on the stretch to **Temple 81: Shiromineji (White Peak Temple)**. But its large compound rewards us with its beautiful forested scenery and a tiny grotto with a spring. This refreshing canvas of nature continues along the route to the next four temples. **Temple 82: Negoroji (Fragrant Root Temple)** is hidden away in the mountains, its main hall framed by a series of corridors containing 33,000 metal Kannon statues donated by devotees. **Temple 83: Ichinomiyaji (First Shrine Temple)** is in the centre of the city of Takamatsu. **Temple 84: Yashimaji (Roof Island Temple)** is on a hill on the north-east coast of Takamatsu City, on an exposed plateau at the summit of Yashima Mountain. **Temple 85: Yakuriji (Eight Chestnuts Temple)**, the next to last mountain temple on the pilgrimage, is located in a valley below the summit.

I quickly consider the temples we have visited on the island. There are hundreds of temples in Shikoku, and some are associated with the 88 pilgrimage temples. But these 88 are the only ones we visit during our eight days here, our gruelling itinerary already bursting at the seams.

I think of how, like the temples in well-known tourist destinations, those here are meant to be more than just impressive edifices. Through them, I have become more aware of the country's history, timeless values and religious and cultural heritage.

I remember visiting popular tourist areas, such as Kyoto, Nikko and Kamakura, where some temples are magnificently constructed around nature with remarkable attention to Japanese craft and material detailing. I have seen singularly impressive and majestic temples. I have been awed over and over again by their grand structures, gilded exteriors and glorious interiors. I have been enraptured by their elaborate courtyards, exquisite gardens and elegant statues.

What a contrast, though, are these 88 temples of Shikoku. I have seen only a few eye-catching vermilion buildings. There have been very few particularly ornate structures. I cannot recall any temple with dramatically grand facades or intricate architecture. I acknowledge that there are some stunning temples with some truly incredible features. But my general sense is that the Shikoku temples are muted in poignant simplicity.

It is this simplicity that draws me into peaceful introspection. In the dimness of the unadorned prayer halls, I find myself more receptive to the play of light and shadow in my interior self. In the bareness of the courtyards, my sensitivity amplifies the glorious creation around me – the mountains, the cedar trees, the sunlight, the wind.

These temples are memorable not because of exceptional aesthetics but because they are part of the Shikoku *henro*.

Lunch is a feast. It is Day 8 of our journey and only the second time in the entire eight-day pilgrimage that we have a proper, though quick, lunch. In the past days, to maximise our time on the road, we have skipped breakfast, grabbed a simple sandwich at a convenience store or *conbini*, for lunch on the go, and nibbled on some snacks in the car to tide us over until dinner.

It is an hour after midday and we are only three temples shy of completing the 88-temple pilgrimage in the eight days, as we initially planned. Thanks to the excellent organising by Katsuji and Mayumi, our spirits are soaring. We are optimistic that we will complete our visits to the remaining temples by late afternoon. That will give us enough time to get to the airport for our evening flight back to Tokyo.

And what a treat lunch is in the self-service roadside restaurant. We indulge in *sanuki udon*, the speciality of Kagawa Prefecture. These tasty thick white noodles with a relatively firm, chewy texture take the name *sanuki* from the old name of Kagawa. It is a classic Japanese dish where these noodles are simmered in a broth with other ingredients such as shrimp, fish or beef.

Before we savour the delicious noodles in the big bowl, we say '*Itadakimasu*' with a slight bow and our hands together. I have always loved this simple aspect of Japanese culture. It is more than the equivalent of 'Bon appetit' or 'Let's eat'. The translation of '*Itadakimasu*' is closer to 'I humbly receive', thereby expressing an appreciation towards all who have made this meal possible, similar to saying grace before meals.

With its roots in ancient Buddhist practices, '*Itadakimasu*' acknowledges the human labour of the farmers, the market intermediaries and the kitchen staff, and Mother Nature for the lives of plants and animals.

Our mood during lunch is carefree and upbeat. We are only hours from finishing our pilgrimage. At that point, we will be able to say that we have completed our visit to the 88 temples in eight days, just as we set out to do. Katsuji, Mayumi and I share our stories excitedly. We exchange our observations and laugh over our minor misadventures. We are grateful that we have a nice warm sit-down lunch together today.

'*Gochisosama*,' we say to each other at the end of our delicious meal. This is a beautiful word whose original meaning is 'May I receive the nourishment from this offering so that my body remains in good health and I can fulfil the good wishes of all beings'.

In modern-day Japan, we utter this word almost perfunctorily, without much thought as to what it means. In essence, however, it conveys beautifully the profound Buddhist teaching of gratitude to all beings who have made possible the partaking of a meal.

When I lived in Hong Kong, colleagues told me that leaving some food on the plate was considered polite behaviour. To consume everything would convey the message that the food served was not enough. In Japan, however, I have heard that children are taught not to leave food on the plate. It is true that this might have been more the case in the past than in present times. Still, leaving food on the plate is seen as demonstrating a lack of respect for the food. Food is acknowledged as being a blessing from Mother Nature. In Japanese, *kome* refers to grains of rice. Written in kanji, it comprises the characters for the numbers eight, ten and eight. Hence, it is said that there are 88 deities in each grain of rice.

Mayumi told me that she often left some rice in her bowl when she was growing up. Her mother would then say, 'One grain has 88 deities. How many deities are you going to ruin?'

And while there is now no pressure to finish all the food on our plates, we consume every last morsel of the *sanuki udon* in our bowls.

Thus, by mid-afternoon, sufficiently nourished and revitalised, we embark upon the final leg of our journey.

I thought we would be driving up the mountain again and am pleasantly surprised that we are travelling downhill as **Temple 86: Shidoji (Temple of Fulfilling One's Wish)** is on the coast. It is a pleasant enough day, and there are *henro* exploring the temple compound. Anxious to be on our way, we make our visit quick. Then we hurry to **Temple 87: Nagaoji (Long Tail Temple)**, with its stone posts announcing 'May Peace Prevail on Earth'. Grey clouds loom on the horizon.

As we approach **Temple 88: Okuboji (Large Hollow Temple)**, the thought of completing the pilgrimage energises us.

Other pilgrims return from Temple 88 to Temple 1, completing the circle. This act of returning to the temple from which you started is called *orei mairi* or thank-you visit. However, for Mayumi, Katsuji and me, Temple 88 is our final stop. After that, we plan to go directly to the airport.

There are two entrance gates to Temple 88, and, standing in front of the one closer to the car park, I feel my heart quickening at the thought that we are now at the threshold of the conclusion of our journey. Part of me wants to hurry through the gateway into the secluded grounds, as a sore-hearted traveller might embrace the delights of a humble refuge in which to rest bruised limbs. Yet, another part of me wants to linger just outside the gate, savouring the precious experiences of the journey, aware that a foot in the temple compound is a step towards completing the pilgrimage.

Framed beautifully by the trees around it and the entrance gates in front, the *hondo* or main hall looks subtly majestic. As we pass the entrance gate, I notice the Japanese flag hoisted above the path leading to the main hall. It fills me with pride to be completing this 88-temple pilgrimage in a country I have grown to love so much.

Although this temple compound is no more impressive than others on the pilgrimage trail, its atmosphere is palpably different. It seems more energetic, more spirited and more vibrant – perhaps because almost every person gathered here is celebrating in some way the completion of their pilgrimage.

At the familiar sight of pilgrims at the washbasin, I recall the 87 times over the last eight days that I have taken the water ladle in my hand to begin the purification ritual. And now this will be my eighty-eighth time. I smile at the collage of memories, and I sense inside me a quiet trusting.

As I observe pilgrims light their candles and protectively place them on the stand, I connect with them, having done the same in all the 88 temples. I feel a deep, affirming warmth within me. Like the happy bus pilgrims streaming by who are excited to pose for a group photo, I too feel more joyful and animated.

Then, by the side of a building, I see a cluster of *kongo-zue* or walking sticks left by pilgrims, and another wave of emotion washes over me. Legend has it that Kobo Daishi left his walking stick at this sacred site. Following his example, pilgrims have made it a tradition to part with their wooden staff here to say farewell to Kobo Daishi and mark the end of their pilgrimage. For a split second, I consider taking my staff back with me to Australia but concede regretfully that it would be logistically challenging. This lesson in non-attachment could not be more concrete. With a heavy heart, I acknowledge what I need to do.

Feeling a trifle subdued, I distractedly make my way to the main hall along with Mayumi. Although the principal deity, Yakushi Nyorai, is not exposed for public viewing, a depiction shows him holding a trumpet shell in his hand instead of a medicine jar. By blowing the trumpet shell, he dissipates the many worries that cloud people's minds.

Mayumi excitedly points at the signboard towards the side of the main hall. The kanji on the board say 'Yakushi Nyorai'. But a part of the kanji is missing, much like a letter with incomplete strokes. This is not a mistake, however, Mayumi assures me. Instead, it is a message that reminds us all that the circuit is never fully completed, that faith never ends. In a way, although we have finished the pilgrimage, it is just the start of another journey.

With my spirits buoyed by this powerful message, we proceed to the temple office to have the last stamp imprinted in crimson red in our *nokyocho*. I feel a sense of achievement as I receive the vermilion stamp in my pilgrim's book. Then I smile broadly as I receive my completion certificate – 88 temples in eight days.

Mayumi, Katsuji and I give each other high-fives as we step outside the temple office. '*Omedetou*. Congratulations,' we repeatedly say to each other. With unrestrained smiles and happy countenances, we are visibly high-spirited, so joyful at having accomplished our mission. But, more importantly, we are grateful that we have each had a fantastic journey on many levels.

The real sense of completion comes when I lay my wooden staff to rest. I remove the brocade cloth cap covering the top of my walking stick and the little silver bell. I ring it one last time before putting these into my sling bag. As is the custom, I have paid the fee of 1,000 yen, approximately $10, to entrust my walking stick to the temple by placing it in a big bin at the doorway of the office. In a designated ceremony that will take place in a couple of months, my walking stick will be burned along with those left by the other pilgrims.

What surprises me is that finally letting go of my walking stick kindles a sense of joy and liberation.

My beautiful *nokyocho*, with its brocade cover of interwoven blue, gold and white threads, is a precious artefact of my personal story on this pilgrimage. This is my one prized possession among everything I have with me today. It holds the vermilion stamps from the 88 sacred sites of Shikoku. Through many epiphanies, it has been with me as I have connected with God in the altar space of sacred creation.

There has been no single moment of big revelation for me, no magic-wand transformation. But there have been profound realisations about my inner journey and a steady outpouring of grace that cleanses the soul and refreshes the spirit. There have been moments when the Divine touched my heart with equally profound power and tenderness.

The message for me is clear – to embrace the present moment, shine my light and walk my path … putting one foot in front of the other, taking one step and then the next … purposefully and with joy. In short, to respond to the invitation to 'come and see'.

Eight-eight temples in eight days.

END OF DAY

ON THE FLIGHT BACK to Tokyo, I think about how pilgrimage is a liminal space – from the Latin *limen* for 'threshold'. It is an in-betweenness. One casts off from ordinary life, interrupting the familiar and mundane routines by venturing into the unknown. The journey takes one to new thresholds that evoke a transcendental experience, resonating as sacred or divine, whatever one's religious beliefs. Between departure and arrival, we find our lives enriched, our experiences enlivened and our horizons broadened. Indeed, I have discovered the Shikoku pilgrimage not as a single destination but as a thousand paths strewn with experiences to be enjoyed, lessons to be learned and pearls of wisdom to be grasped.

For my part, I am deeply blessed to have had the perfect companions for this trip – Katsuji with his excellent driving, his fun-loving ways and his endearing sense of humour, and Mayumi for her generosity of spirit, her deep knowledge of Japanese history and culture and her warm friendship. They make real to me the quote from the Italian writer Luciano De Crescenzo: 'We are each of us angels with only one wing, and we can only fly by embracing one another.' I could not have asked for better tour guides and companions.

Before boarding the flight, they surprise me with a small present – a simple black canvas tote, just like Mayumi's. I didn't realise that they had bought one for me as well, at the temple store.

I look at the number 88, written in big white letters. Then I look at the line below that says 'Life is *HENRO*'. And then a profound realisation grips me. What if my whole life is a liminal space? What if, at the heart of my essence as a human being, I am a pilgrim? What then? I may already have known that in some way. But sometimes it takes a journey like this to draw us back into that remembrance and its significance in a deeply visceral way.

What now? Well, I will inhabit my life in a way that is deeply felt and fully breathed. In such a way that all my heartbeats bring me closer to my God. And, one day, beyond where the footpath ends, He will lead me home.

III

THE RETURN HOME

Monks

and

Mysteries

KOYASAN

MAYUMI, KATSUJI AND I meet up in June 2019, a month after the Shikoku pilgrimage. We fly from Tokyo to Osaka, where we rent a car to drive to Koyasan. In keeping with *henro* tradition, our visit is to thank Kobo Daishi for our safety and protection throughout the pilgrimage and to report its successful completion.

A trip to Osaka at any other time would not have been complete without a visit to Dotonbori, a bustling tourist mecca famous for its dazzling neon signs and enticing food districts. This time, however, a different excitement is in the air. Katsuji inspects the rental car while Mayumi and I review our itinerary for our road trip to Koyasan.

Our meandering two-hour ride from carefree, relaxed Osaka to sacred Koyasan is a tranquil ascent towards the shaded brilliance of the morning light streaming through heavily wooded slopes of pines. The road curves, then climbs again, a luminescence gently enveloping the landscape. I love these peaceful road trips that transport me into the quiet space of my heart.

As the road weaves through the thick forests, I find myself increasingly light-hearted. We round the final bend and I glimpse my smile in the reflection in the car window. Indeed, I can hardly wait to set foot once again in this place steeped in sacred history, shielded in mystery.

Just up the road, marking the entrance to the sanctuary that is Koyasan, is the massive two-storey vermilion structure called Daimon Gate, first built in 1141 C.E. An impressive five sections make up the enormous carved gateway to the city of Kobo Daishi, with the middle sections flanked on both sides by the muscular, wrestler-like temple guard statues.

I excitedly walk through the centre opening. I am struck not so much by the imposing size and structures of this towering edifice as by the beauty of the glorious skies and the magnificence of the verdant landscape that lie beyond it. Entering Koyasan is itself a kind of a rite of passage. It reveals itself with a humble majesty unfolding in silent splendour.

There is a quiet power and a beauty in this place that we cannot help but notice and respect, whatever our religious orientations or beliefs.

The story of Koyasan goes back to the early ninth century. Through his studies in China, Kukai had mastered the mysteries of esoteric or tantric Buddhism that came to be known by the Japanese name Shingon Buddhism or 'True Word'. Upon his return to Japan, he sought to set up a training centre where its teachings and practices could flourish.

A remarkable legend tells us how Koyasan came to be that centre.[1] It is said that one day, about a decade after Kukai began his quest for the right site, he awoke from a deep meditative trance. In the far-off wilderness he saw standing beside him a hunter with one white dog and one black dog. This hunter was named Kariba Myojin and was the patron deity of Koyasan. The hunter led him up to a remote, heavily wooded area. In one of the trees, Kukai found the *sanko* (Buddhist ceremonial tool) that he had hurled with incredible force from a beach in China before returning to Japan. He took

> Mountains have a way of inspiring, renewing, transforming.
> Here, I do not feel that I have to grasp for the Divine,
> for the Divine has been waiting for me all along
> and readily draws me unto Itself.

that as clear confirmation that this was the right place to establish his meditation retreat centre. It was only a matter of time before Koyasan fully blossomed as the birthplace of Shingon Buddhism.

We stroll through the slow-paced town, which is spread out along the main road for about 3.5 kilometres, running from east to west. In the distance I see the Chumon Gate, its red, white and green exterior still radiant under the ominously dimming clouds. Passing through it, we find ourselves in the sprawling sacred precinct of the Danjo Garan temple complex.

I survey the vast monastic compound. It is said to be composed of 19 or 20 structures, which include, among other things, a memorial hall and three pagodas. So this is where the secret Shingon Buddhism training has been taking place for hundreds of years, I think. I cannot help but feel as though we have stepped into the pages of a centuries-old storybook where places and events come alive in the unfolding drama seeded by Kobo Daishi's vision.

I pause in front of Kondo Hall, home to the enshrined image of Yakushi Nyorai, the Medicine Master Buddha. I wonder what ceremonies have been held in this large, wood-covered, reinforced-concrete building.

Hardly have I had time to ponder this when my attention is unexpectedly seized by the towering crimson *tahoto*, a Buddhist architectural structure in the form of a Japanese pagoda, beside it. In the centre of the impressive, almost 49-metre-high Konpon Daito Pagoda is an enormous statue of Dainichi Nyorai, the Cosmic Buddha, considered to be the personification of Ultimate Reality. I am not quite sure what that means. Around the pagoda's interior, surrounding

Dainichi Nyorai, is a unique iconography of elegant statues and bright paintings on pillars that create the edifying, myth-like atmosphere of a mandala used in ceremonial rituals.

Kobo Daishi is credited with having initiated the construction of the Kondo Hall and the Daito Pagoda, with his successors completing them. Over time, through his successors' work, several halls and pagodas were added to the complex, including the Toto (Eastern Pagoda), Saito (Western Pagoda) and Koya Myojin Shrine, a Shinto shrine that honours the local *kami* – the Shinto gods – of Mount Koya. Here also can be found the exquisite Reihokan Museum, which conserves various Buddhist cultural assets belonging to the temples of Koyasan. It boasts an extensive collection of Buddhist paintings, sculptures, ritual and ceremonial implements, fine calligraphic documents and sutras, as well as related archaeological objects.

Mayumi's voice calling out to Katsuji and me is a welcome distraction. My gaze follows the direction in which she is pointing. There is another hall, called Miedo (Great Portrait Hall), that houses a painting of Kobo Daishi and is open to visitors only one day a year. But that is not what Mayumi is pointing at.

'The *sanko-no-matsu*,' she exclaims, and I understand immediately that she is referring to the pine tree standing in front of the Great Portrait Hall. This is the tree in which Kukai's *sanko* miraculously landed, or so it is said, after he threw it from China.

As if to mark the significance of our discovery, we hear a deep 'gong!' ring out and we hasten towards it. At the bell tower, I watch transfixed as a monk in a black robe gracefully manoeuvres himself into a backwards-leaning position as he deftly pulls on the chain attached to the copper Daito Bell, Japan's fourth-largest bell. Each deep 'gong!' reverberates solemnly through the compound.

I am just about to sit on a rock, content to listen for a few more minutes to the ringing of the bell, but only metres away I notice a commotion, and soon we are swept up in the energy of a small crowd standing by the roadside to witness a joyful parade.

Unbeknown to us when we booked this trip to Koyasan weeks ago, today is an important date. On the fifteenth of June is held the Aoba Matsuri, a festival of ceremonies commemorating the birth of Kobo Daishi. The highlight is a procession in which a portable shrine with statues of him as a child and him as an adult is paraded across the town. Adults and schoolchildren join in the singing and dancing to honour their town's founder.

At the tail end of the procession, we make our way to Kongobuji (Diamond Peak Temple), the head monastery of the Shingon sect. I tiptoe respectfully through the exposed wooden corridors, looking into the elegant rooms with gilded sliding doors and picturesque walls painted with cranes and seasonal flowers and plum trees. I am fascinated by the paintings depicting Kobo Daishi's journey to China and his subsequent founding of Koyasan.

The deck opens up to a viewing point of the well-preserved Banryutei Rock Garden, the largest of its sort in Japan. Set across the 2,340-square-metre area are 100 granite slabs configured to suggest a male and female dragon emerging from a sea of clouds to protect the temple. I am impressed by the quiet majesty of the garden, my gaze meandering down the patterns of the raked gravel. Sitting here on the front porch of the Okuden (Inner Hall), we are blessed to be in the best viewing position. Ordinarily, visitors would not have access to this area. An exception is made only on the fifteenth of June, Kobo Daishi's birthday.

Kobo Daishi left this earthly life in 835 C.E. and was interred on the eastern peak of Koyasan. But it is clear that his legacy lives on.

Meanwhile, the skies have opened and the heavy rains forecast for the day soak the land. Reports in the evening news say that the rain had been coming down in torrents, apparently the heaviest rainfall yet this year. It is, therefore, surprising that there was only the slightest whisper of a shower during the festival parade. The unrestrained deluge was unleashed only after the festivities had concluded. An Aoba Matsuri miracle, some say – it never rains during the procession to celebrate the birth of Kobo Daishi.

I chuckle to myself as I recall an anecdote about the meaning of heavy rains in Koyasan. It is said that eating fish or meat is prohibited here. So a torrential downpour is necessary to cleanse this mystical mountain of the impurity left by visitors who eat fish and meat.

It is just as well, then, that we have booked our accommodation for the evening in a *shukubo* or temple lodging that serves fully vegan Buddhist meals. One of the highlights of the visit for pilgrims and tourists is the opportunity to stay the night in an austere yet often richly historic temple. *Shukubo* lack the modern conveniences of contemporary hotels. Their unique offering is a glimpse into the ascetic life of Buddhist monks,

> Miracles happen when the extraordinary is made visible in the seemingly ordinary. I need only notice these to celebrate the sacrament of wonder.
> But, oftentimes, my busyness and preoccupations shackle me to inattention.

even a chance to join them in morning prayers or meditation. Of the 117 or so temples in Koyasan, slightly more than 50 accommodate overnight guests.

The tranquil atmosphere of Koyasan is the perfect setting for our *shukubo* experience in Sekishoin, a temple with a long and esteemed history. Rectangular lattice-work panels slide open to reveal my simple room in the style of a traditional Japanese inn called a *ryokan*. It is enveloped in a comfortable stillness. The traditional Japanese bedding, a futon set consisting of a floppy, cotton-filled mattress and a soft, velvety, brocade-edged duvet, lies on one side of the tatami-mat floor, a sort of woven-reed matting that feels gentle and firm underfoot.

Sliding paper doors with wooden frames open onto a small, glass-enclosed sitting area that looks out onto a captivating scene of maple and cedar trees in a small area of the courtyard. It exudes beauty and serenity. This breathtaking piece of restful nature sits just outside my room, no doubt a tiny corner of the temple's vast garden, which spreads across 6,611 square metres. A little plot of heaven, I am inclined to think. The perfect setting for quiet prayer and meditation.

A maze of corridors, with *uguisubari* or wooden 'nightingale' floors that creak or make a chirping sound when walked on, connects the guest rooms to the large hall where meals are served and, further on, to the ornately decorated prayer room. Interestingly, these creaking floors remind me of another temple, frequently referred to as the Ninja Temple (Ninjadera or Myouryuji), in Kanazawa, which has trap doors, secret passageways and creaking floors that alert inhabitants to any intruder.

Breakfast and dinner are prepared and served by the monks in assigned halls. The meals are eaten not with the monks but with other guests lining the length of the room on opposite sides, facing each other. Small bowls with an assortment of vegetable and tofu-based dishes, accompanied by rice and miso soup, are arranged in a wooden lacquer tray set a few centimetres off the floor.

One highlight of our *shukubo* stay is the Buddhist meal, *shojin ryori*. It has no animal products at all, consists of five flavours (tangy, sweet, sour, salty and fermented), five colours (red, yellow, blue-green, black and white) and five methods of cooking (raw, boiled, baked or grilled, fried and steamed). It is said to be literally 'a diet in pursuit of enlightenment'.[2]

The recipes for this vegan cuisine have been handed down through generations of monks over the 1,100-year history of this *shukubo*. My favourite is *goma dofu* (sesame tofu), a smooth and silky panna-cotta-like delicacy made from finely ground sesame seeds and *kuzu* flour. Its flavour is enhanced with just a sprinkle of soy and a dash of fresh *wasabi* (Japanese horseradish). Katsuji likes *goma dofu* too, so we exchange smiles when we see that this is one of the dishes in our dinner tray.

Shojin ryori is rich in textures and subtle in flavours. 'It is a delicate, beautifully plated, gently seasoned, hearty meal,' I remark to Mayumi with genuine appreciation.

The other highlight of our *shukubo* stay is the early-morning Buddhist service in the prayer hall. Feeble light from ornamental Japanese lanterns casts delicate shadows across the room, lifting the sombre mood with its soft luminescence. Thick clouds of incense rise gracefully from the lighted sticks. The monks chant the Heart Sutra in unison, their deeply resonant tones at times punctuated by the striking of a bell or a sonorous drum. I join my voice with theirs as I follow through the romanised version of the syllables on the printout distributed earlier by a young monk.

'Oh, you know the Heart Sutra,' a monk says to us in halting English after the prayer service, dismissing my protestations as mere modesty. 'Are you going to Shikoku?' he asks. He is excited when he learns that we have just completed the Shikoku pilgrimage. He seems even gladder when I tell him that I have come to Koyasan all the way from Australia.

I have consistently elicited this kind of reaction throughout this trip whenever people hear where I have come from. I am touched that people recognise the effort involved in such a long-haul trip and are genuinely pleased that I am drawn to their land.

As we get ready to check out of the *shukubo*, I take one last look at the two big colourful square posters hanging prominently in the hall. Having seen them in other temples before, I know they are the Kongokai Mandala (Mandala of the Diamond Realm) and the Taizokai Mandala (Mandala of the Womb Realm). Together, the pair make a unified set called Ryokai Mandala (Mandala of the Two Realms or the Two Worlds). They embody the central devotional images that explain the world of Esoteric Buddhism practice in Japan.[3]

I do not know much about the details of these mandalas, only that they represent the Buddhist view of the universe and are central to Shingon Buddhism rituals. I do not fully comprehend the Heart Sutra, only that it contains the kernel of Buddhist teachings in its 14 lines. I do not have a deep understanding of Buddhism, only that as a philosophy it carries practical and empowering wisdom about how life is to be lived.

But I am curious to learn about our respective religious traditions. I am eager to listen to the stories of people who have lived the ever-unfolding meanings of their faith. As I do so, I begin to see unmistakably that when we expand the radius of our acceptance and respect, the world becomes a better, kinder, more just place.

We leave Sekishoin and walk towards Okunoin, the vast cemetery whose highlight is the mausoleum of Kobo Daishi.

Along the way, we stop by Karukayado, another temple that is not too far away. It was in this temple in 2017 that I bought, as a souvenir of my first trip to Koyasan, a simple bracelet with a single strand of little orange beads connected to a small silver *gokosho* (a five-pronged *vajra*), a Buddhist ritual tool representing the indestructibility of Buddhist Law, firmness of spirit and spiritual power. It goes quite nicely with the brightly coloured bracelet of plaited strings given to guests at Sekishoin.

Karukayado has its own touching folk legend. It is said that in the twelfth century there was a little boy named Ishidomaru from a faraway province who, along with his mother, went to

> My experience tells me that silence creates the space for deep inner listening, that there is a mystery that is essential to faith, that stories of a living faith are really an invitation to acknowledge that life itself is a precious gift, that, when I am humble, tender and open, I more readily receive the Giver of that gift.

Koyasan in search of his long-lost father, who had renounced the world. Since precepts prohibited women from entering the sacred mountain, his mother stayed at a lodging located at the foot of Koyasan. While awaiting the return of Ishidomaru, she suddenly became ill and breathed her last.

It so happened that Ishidomaru met a Buddhist monk, Karukaya Doshin, who turned out to be the father he was yearning to see. However, the monk did not divulge his identity to his son and, while he did not acknowledge their relationship, the monk accepted Ishidomaru as his companion in the hermitage. Legend has it that father and son lived, studied and practised asceticism together for 40 years without Ishidomaru ever finding out that the monk was his father.

A more poignant version of the story is that, for the entire 40 years that they practised in the hermitage together, Karukaya Doshin did not realise that Ishidomaru was his own son.

As a mother, my heart aches as Mayumi recounts this sad story to me, reading the Japanese explanation that accompanies the temple paintings depicting the story of Ishidomaru and his father. This story reminds me once again of Kudoyama, a town located in Ito District, which we passed on our way to Koyasan.

The name 'Kudoyama' can be literally translated as 'Nine Times Mountain'. Once again, it talks about how, in ancient times, women were not allowed on sacred mountains. They were prohibited from even entering the forest or approaching the holy temples. The same was true for Kobo Daishi's mother, who could not visit him when he started the temple in Mount Koya. Hence Kobo Daishi had to make the trip down the mountain nine times a month to visit his mother.

As we look at the paintings, a man comes in and engages us in conversation. It turns out that he is the resident monk at Karukayado. Looking at me, he says in Japanese, 'I remember you,' as Mayumi translates. I am surprised that, somehow, he has recognised me from my visit two years back, though I am not sure why he would remember me, and he does not elaborate.

He is not dressed in any intricate ochre robes befitting the dignity of his office but looks quite ordinary in his sports shirt and dark trousers. His jovial nature becomes evident from the moment he invites us to join him for coffee. He entertains us for close to an hour with his amusing stories.

He tells us about his previous life as a policeman in Tokyo and how he is now thinking of going back because it gets too cold in Koyasan in the winter. Translating his stories into English for me, Mayumi says that he is what one might call '*Edoko*' or 'a child of Edo', someone who was born and raised in Tokyo.

Having enjoyed the coffee, the heartwarming banter and the interesting stories, we begin to take our leave. The monk gives Mayumi and me a small Jizo statue to show his gratitude for our having visited Karukayado temple. I've noticed that little Jizo statues are spread all around the inner ledges of the temple.

Mayumi buys a packet of incense sticks for us to offer in Okunoin and I enquire about making a small donation to the temple. In his characteristically good-natured manner, the monk says that they do not accept money as a donation. Instead of money, he says with a big laugh, people usually donate things like *sake* (rice wine).

Katsuji, Mayumi and I exit the temple into the wonderful light of day, feeling much more cheerful and high-spirited from this lovely encounter with a happy, down-to-earth monk who was previously a policeman in Tokyo.

I think again of our conversation with this monk. It was in Japanese, with Mayumi translating into English for me and conveying my comments back in Japanese. It is not unlikely that something might have been lost in translation, but I have nevertheless felt that a beautiful human connection was present there. While the words may have been lacking, I have always found the heartwarming authenticity of a genuine human encounter to be deeply compelling.

'This is the memorial for Takeda Shingen and Takeda Katsuyori,' Mayumi announces excitedly as we begin to stroll through Okunoin. 'Oh, and look, that is for the seventh Tokugawa shogun, Tokugawa Ietsugu,' she exclaims. 'And this one is for Date Masamune, who founded the city of Sendai.'

She rattles off a litany of names as she explores the other memorials, patiently explaining to me their historical significance.

I feel as though we are walking down a history hall of fame – but we are, in fact, strolling along the 2-kilometre cobbled pathway of the Ichi-no-hashi Bridge, the traditional entrance to Okunoin. Mayumi is pointing out mossy tombstones and eroded memorials along the way.

Since I first came here in 2017, I've been looking forward to visiting Okunoin again. With its more than 200,000 gravestones, memorials and monuments, Okunoin is not only a vast forest graveyard but also a place of worship and deep contemplation. At the end of Ichi-no-hashi Bridge is the Gobyo-no-hashi Bridge, which connects to the famed mausoleum of Kobo Daishi.

Even if one is not of a religious bent, a trip to this most remarkable site is guaranteed to be memorable. I have come to appreciate Okunoin even more deeply having read Nicoloff's beautiful and detailed description in his book *Sacred Kōyasan*.

On night-time tours led by English-speaking monks, the descending mist often eclipses the cobbled walkway and the gravestones that flank it. Ancient cedars of dizzying heights conspire with stone lanterns to cast eerie shadows in the dim yellow light. Crumbling stone-faced statues, rising from centuries-old obscurity, hover near multi-tiered stupas and weathered monuments, peering through the thick foliage, as they have done, season after season, century after century, for more than 1,000 years.

Yet, for all its unearthly, mysterious ambiance, Okunoin – even at night – is a place of unalterable, indestructible peace and tranquillity.

It seems as if Okunoin has changed but little since my last visit. A sense of serenity pervades our morning stroll. Mayumi continues to point out the tombstones and memorials of emperors, shoguns, feudal lords and military commanders that all stand at attention in the company of ancient cedar, cypress, red pine, hemlock fir and umbrella pine trees.

'These historical figures fought each other when they were alive, but it seems they have become friends posthumously,' Mayumi says, offering insight.

At a secondary entrance to Okunoin are gravestones that look more recent, along with huge granite or marble monuments that large companies have erected in honour of their deceased employees. The highly recognisable names include Nissan, Sharp, Panasonic and Kubota.

There are some rather unusual memorials as well. Take, for instance, the rocket-shaped one built by an aviation company. Or the one shaped like a coffee cup belonging to a famous coffee company. What I find most curious, however, is the memorial that a pest company built in honour of all the termites that have been exterminated through the use of its products.

Katsuji and I keep step with Mayumi, noticing Jizo statues lining the sides of the path or watching from atop stone monuments, like guards standing at attention.

I remember the first time I traipsed around Okunoin. My companion said to me, 'Come with me around the corner. I want to show you a statue of the Cosmetic Buddha.'

'You probably mean the Cosmic Buddha, right?' I replied.

'No, the Cosmetic Buddha,' she insisted, pointing to a smiling Jizo statue with rosy cheeks and red lips. On the ground in front of the Jizo were small offerings of cosmetic items, made in the belief that the act would bestow on the giver enhanced beauty and youthfulness.

This time around, I am even more aware of the Jizo statues. They are in the crevices of tree trunks, in the crooks of sturdy branches and clustered in mounds. There must be hundreds if not thousands of them, spread throughout Okunoin.

Along Nakanoshi, another bridge about midway to Gobyo-no-hashi Bridge, some fascinating discoveries unfold.

I walked this exact pathway when I first visited Koyasan in 2017, and now our stroll brings back memories of that first experience.

Two years ago, I refused to look into the well called Sugatami no Ido (Well of Reflections or Mirror Well). It is said that if you fail to see your reflection in the well, death will come upon you in a few years. Mayumi, ever brave, leaps forward to see her reflection in the well. Spurred on by her, I approach the well tentatively, and am relieved to recognise my reflection in the clear water surface, despite my messy hair and shiny nose.

Beside the well is a shrine of Asekaki Jizo, who is forever sweating beneath the burden of the suffering of others. Ah, this I remember well. On my first visit to Koyasan, our monk guide encouraged our small tour group to shake the little bell rope dangling in front of the statue, to call attention to our presence. Then he encouraged us to leave our burdens with this sweating Jizo made of a dark granite.

'Come back tomorrow,' our monk guide said, 'and if you see this statue perspiring as it usually does, you can be assured that he has taken your sufferings upon himself.'

We then come to Kakubanzaka (Kakuban Slope), where it is said that anyone who falls down the slope will die within three years. I smile as I wonder silently to myself if this warning is simply a veiled way to get people to be more careful as they negotiate this tricky slope. It seems that everyone does slow down, paying closer attention to their steps when they reach this part of the path.

At Kakubanzaka, what I discover is an intriguing 90-centimetre memorial to a Buddhist nun named Zenni Jochi. I did not notice this on my previous visit here. Rumour has it that by placing one's ear on the hollow of the monument, one is able to hear either the cries in hell or a voice from heaven. I do not care to confirm or deny the rumour.

My attention is then drawn to a monument to which is clipped several small toy koalas waving the Australian flag. It turns out to be a memorial to the soldiers of Japan and Australia who were deployed to North Borneo and died during the Second World War. The flags of these three countries – Japan, Malaysia and Australia – are flown at the memorial. This is meaningful to me, as an Australian.

As we pass the Gokusho Offering Hall in the Okunoin grounds, I am ecstatic to get one final vermilion stamp for my *nokyocho* – this, in addition to the 88 stamps we already received in Shikoku – truly marking the end of our pilgrimage. My excitement now builds to a crescendo as I see the Gobyo-no-hashi Bridge in the distance. We are approaching the pinnacle of our Okunoin experience – the visit to the mausoleum of Kobo Daishi.

Mayumi rushes along to a crowd gathering by the public plaza before the bridge. As I quicken my pace, she explains the excitement around. As Kobo Daishi is believed not to have died but to be simply resting in eternal meditation, meals are still lovingly and ritually prepared for him at 6 a.m. and 10:30 a.m. every day. Today, our timing is perfect – it is just coming up to 10:30 a.m.

We arrive just as the food is being brought out of the kitchen and the chief monk in his ochre robe takes it to a small shrine housing Ajimi Jizo, the Taste-Testing Jizo.

The food, found satisfactory, is then placed in a huge wooden box and set on the shoulders of the monks. They walk slowly, solemnly, with the chief monk leading them in the *shojingu* procession that is the ceremony of bringing meals to Kobo Daishi. Apparently, only the chief monk is allowed to serve the meals.

'What food is prepared for Kobo Daishi?' I wonder aloud.

'Kobo Daishi is so progressive. I am sure he would not mind even a meal of spaghetti,' Mayumi asserts, making me grin.

Following the other pilgrims before us – and as tradition says we should – we straighten our attire so as to be at our most presentable. Then we put our hands together and bow in reverence in the direction of Kobo Daishi's mausoleum, just as we did before we set foot on the Ichi-no-hashi Bridge. We then proceed to cross the Gobyo-no-hashi Bridge.

Gobyo-no-hashi Bridge marks the start of the innermost sanctum, the hallowed ground for the sacred mausoleum of Kobo Daishi and, thus, the holiest place in Okunoin. Beyond that point, photography, eating, drinking and smoking are strictly prohibited.

The monks with the huge wooden box containing the meal of Kobo Daishi begin to ascend a flight of steps. As we follow them, we see the Torodo Hall (Hall of Lamps or Lantern Hall) emerging through the trees in the distance. This great pavilion is Okunoin's main hall for worship, built in front of Kobo Daishi's mausoleum.

'I'd say that, for Japanese people, Kobo Daishi is our number one, surpassing all others,' Mayumi declares.

I look at her quizzically.

'There are several schools of Buddhism in Japan, and, like in any other religious tradition, there are conflicts among those schools. Adherents of one Buddhist sect may reject members of other sects,' she explains. 'But everyone loves Kobo Daishi, even if they don't necessarily belong to the Shingon sect. That's what I mean when I say that Kobo Daishi is our number one.'

I nod my head in assent.

She reminds me that we can see the evidence at Okunoin, with its memorial towers and tombs of historical figures. 'It's interesting to see the tombs of those who fought against each other placed side by side with their enemies,' Mayumi continues. 'Kobo Daishi accepts everyone, regardless of the sect to which they belonged or the deeds they committed when they were alive.'

I have had many interesting conversations with Mayumi about religion. Today, she once again affirms views that I have heard previously from many of my Japanese colleagues.

'Japanese people are generally seen as Buddhists by foreigners,' Mayumi tells me. 'But most of us are not conscious of religion at all. Since the Meiji Restoration of 1868, when the new government destroyed temples in order to separate Shinto from Buddhism, temples have become just places in which to hold funeral services. But people still want to have something that can give them the emotional support to live better. Both Buddhism and Shinto are deeply rooted in our daily lives as a kind of philosophy rather than a religion.'

My own observation is that the idea of religion as such is quite ambiguous for Japanese people. How often have I heard it said that the Japanese celebrate birth and early-years milestones with Shinto services, may opt for a Christian wedding ceremony, and then will have Buddhist funeral rites at the end of their life. I am no longer surprised by this. John Dougill, a British professor at Ryukoku University in Kyoto, insightfully notes a key contrast in perspectives. He remarks that, while Christians seek a singular truth, the Japanese pursue multiple truths. Intriguingly, he points out, the Japanese language doesn't differentiate between singular and plural forms.[4]

'The many and varied influences that Buddhism and Shinto have on people's lives', Mayumi continues, 'have resulted in the nurturing of a unique sense of balance in Japanese people. Because the basic concepts are not that different from each other, people can share a mutual connection even when their paths are divergent. Even today, people from different schools of Buddhism practise Shikoku *henro*, hoping to receive some merit from Buddha, the *bosatsu* and Kobo Daishi, regardless of the sect to which they belong.'

Finally, we arrive at the Lantern Hall, which has several sections. From our seats close to one end, we see the gently flickering light of the 10,000 lanterns filtering through solemnly while the golden-robed monks begin to chant rhythmically in unison. The lamps, donated by devotees in memory of their departed loved ones, are kept permanently illuminated.

The mythical and the historical are intertwined in ancient stories, legends and folklore. Legend has it that two lanterns have been burning continuously for close to a thousand years now. One lantern is said to have been donated by an emperor. It is unclear whether the other was presented by a priest or by an anonymous peasant who sold her hair to buy it and offer it for her deceased parents.

We inch our way to the rear of the hall, across from which is Kobo Daishi's mausoleum. At the entrance of the mausoleum are golden lotus flowers on the right side and on the left.

The spectacular scene of lights and sound and movement in the daytime is nothing short of mesmerising. Although the Lantern Hall is closed in the evenings, memories from my first visit to Koyasan in 2017 flood my mind. I recall the experience of stillness and peace as I stood in the obscure darkness beneath the soft lantern light, which produced a hypnotic effulgence. The strains of the monotone chanting of a lone voice – that of the monk who guided us on the Okunoin night-time tour – had a haunting beauty that I still recall to this day. I remember how I said my own prayers in Koyasan, asking that I might be allowed to return sometime soon. Perhaps this moment is the exact answer to that prayer.

Here on Koyasan there is a sense of the sacred, the mysterious, the transcendent that hovers just on the edge of awareness. Its ethereal quality is perceptible but not fully discernible. This may seem enigmatic to the logical mind, but I feel that it can still be sensed or comprehended by the receptive heart.

We spend what seems to be an endless number of minutes just standing there with our heads bowed.

Our thanks and our report to Kobo Daishi done, we head back to the car in silence. I begin to vaguely recall a beautiful poem about light that so aptly expresses my inner thoughts and sentiments. The first stanza of 'Lead, Kindly Light' by St John Henry Newman (1801–1890) says it all so well:

> Lead, Kindly Light, amid the encircling gloom,
> Lead Thou me on;
> The night is dark, and I am far from home,
> Lead Thou me on.
> Keep Thou my feet;
> I do not ask to see the distant scene;
> One step enough for me.

The last lines echo in my heart:

> I do not ask to see the distant scene;
> One step enough for me.

One step enough for me.

Promise

and

Possibility

SYDNEY

Australia

> A horse is galloping down the road, its rider in a rush.
> A man standing by the roadside calls out, 'Where are you going in such a hurry?'
> 'I don't know,' the rider calls out. 'Ask the horse.'
>
> *Unknown*

FOR A LONG STRETCH of time, I buried myself in the stultifying busyness that dominated the rhythm of my passing days. I enjoyed the excitement of working – I felt incredibly alive when I was travelling and using my gifts of teaching, speaking and storytelling wherever they were needed. But I was also dangerously close to burnout. I felt my days were being swept away by habitual but unproductive routines, mindless activities and unwitting choices. I longed to break away from it all through some experience that would allow me to discover a new dimension of life.

From a weekend trip to Koyasan some years ago, Shikoku beckoned. A casual curiosity soon blossomed into an intense interest. But it was the unsettling experience of a significant life transition that triggered the determined pursuit of that pilgrimage.

I thought I needed a distraction, a diversion from troubling circumstances of uncomfortable career and life shifts.

But the sacred has a way of seeping into even the tiniest cracks in the corridors of our hearts and minds. Looking back, I can see how exploring the outer world reanimated my inner world. And a most surprising twist happened on those trails.

This was a surprise that could only have been divinely orchestrated by, to quote a favourite saying of my mother's, 'a God who writes straight with crooked lines'. For along this

Buddhist route I experienced a reconciliation of my heart with the essential truths of my Christian faith. Paraphrasing the powerfully simple words of Rumi, I wandered from place to place hunting for a necklace of diamonds. But it was already around my neck.

I realised with a new certainty that all my many journeys have had at their core one truth – the yearning for my true eternal home. Claiming this as my reference point, I felt more centred, more grounded, more expansive. And feeling more expansive, I could more easily forgive and release past hurts, sorrows and regrets. I could recognise new strengths and deliberately make empowering choices. I had not attained enlightenment on the journey. But I had gained a new perspective and felt I could greet gladly the changing seasons of my life. I was home.

In Shikoku, I trod the ancient trails of the outer landscape. It manifested three realities: impermanence, incompleteness and imperfection. I recognise these as the hallmarks of the Japanese way of life called *wabi-sabi*. These, too, are the inescapable conditions of our earthly existence: nothing lasts, nothing is finished, and nothing is perfect.

This deepened awareness brought a shift in my inner landscape. These lessons from the pilgrimage do not simply belong in the distant past. They have the power to birth new insights that nourish, nurture and sustain me on my life journey. Indeed, as the poet R.S. Thomas suggests, 'the point of travelling is not to arrive, but to return home laden with pollen you shall work up into honey the mind feeds on'.

All things pass away. The powerful Japanese concept of *ichi-go ichi-e* translates as 'one time, one encounter'. Every encounter is unique. Once a moment slips away, it is forever gone.

I recognise that I can still look wistfully at the past or longingly into the future, but the time I spend on those two shores of experience takes me away from the treasure that is here and now. Once I release any attachments to the past or expectations about the future, I find that there is only now.

Bring your presence to the present, I tell myself. All things pass away. Only God remains. This powerful filter functions to direct my time and my choices.

The incompleteness of the kanji written on the signboard of Okuboji, Temple 88, left a lasting impression on me. Tangibly, this conveyed to me the rhythm at the heart of the universe – that is, the journey never truly ends. What seems to be an ending ushers in yet another new beginning.

When I returned from my travels to Shikoku, I experienced greater clarity of vision. I embraced the promise of possibility more joyfully in the series of new beginnings.

'Let go and let God,' I tell myself. This prodding does not mean passivity but rather active cooperation with the inner promptings of the Spirit of wisdom.

Imperfection is the natural condition of all things, all beings and all of nature. Nature's cycles of inevitable ageing, decay and erosion are visible in the appearance of many of the Shikoku temples, and the evidence of the passage of time and of timelessness within their walls. Yet here too is a compelling invitation to look beyond the surface value of things and to contemplate the beauty of what exists beyond simply the manifest reality.

This attitude allows me to see that beauty need not be flawless to be appreciated. And imperfection can be celebrated for its simple honesty.

This does not mean that I no longer strive for perfection. What it does mean is that I no longer fret over my inadequacies but instead place a more harmonious balance between doing and being and, indeed, becoming.

From the insights gleaned with every step in my Shikoku pilgrimage, I gained new strength and optimism to navigate my experiences today. With the passage of time comes perspective and the recognition that my journey left me forever changed in great and small ways.

There are still days when it feels as though I am the rider on the horse galloping down the road – times when my days get swept away by habitual but unproductive routines, mindless activities and unwitting choices. Such is being human. But I now purposefully 'take back the reins of that horse ride', so to speak, by punctuating my day with simple practices like prayer and meditation, a refreshing nature stroll, or a moment's pause to appreciate beauty and express gratitude.

All healing, it is said, takes place in the pause between the exhale and the inhale. The exhale creates the space for the next abundant inhale. Reminiscing about my pilgrimage experiences in the writing of this book was my healing pause in the time of the Covid-19 pandemic. Now, more mindfully, I embrace the breath that is life. I receive it gratefully and let it nourish me. Then I let it go, gently and lovingly. And as I do, I know that it will come back even more abundant, ever fresh, ever new – with the gift of life's promise and possibility, whether here or beyond.

My wish is that *Shikoku Wisdom for the Wayfarer* has delivered on my intention: to give hope and inspiration in the face of the impermanence, the incompleteness and the imperfection in this journey of life. Perhaps it might even plant a seed of curiosity, if not desire, to visit Shikoku's 88 sacred sites. If so, then this book has accomplished far more than I would ever have imagined.

What I truly know is that I can revisit the wisdom of my experience of Shikoku *henro* at any time or place and allow it once again to nourish and nurture my spirit. It is there for me always.

旅程

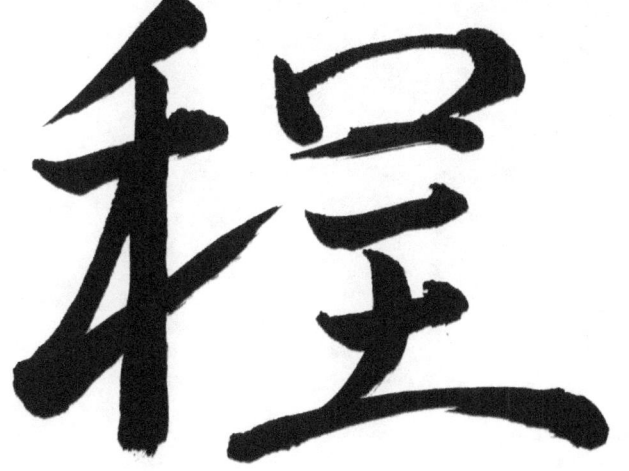

IV

OUR ITINERARY: BY CAR TO 88 TEMPLES IN 8 DAYS

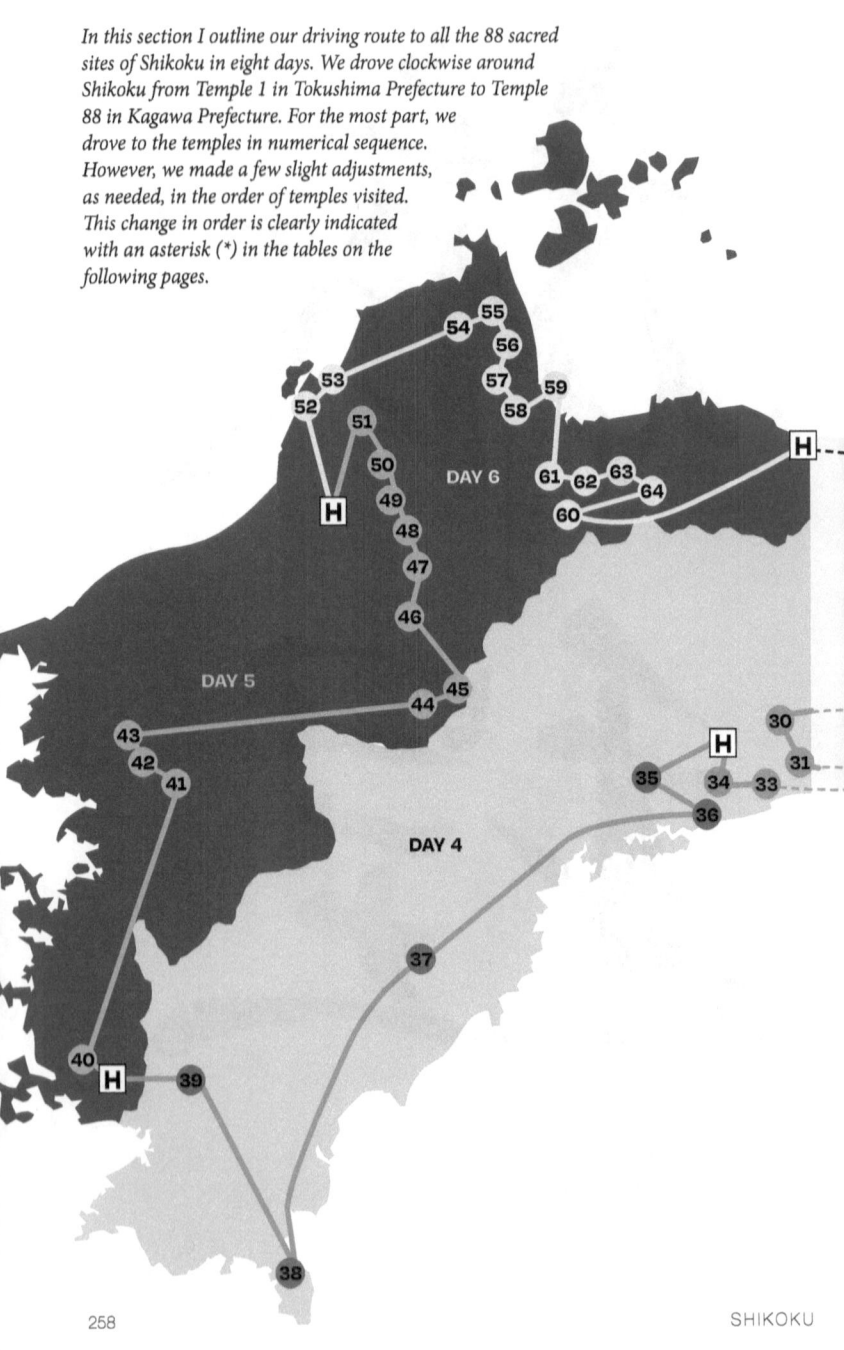

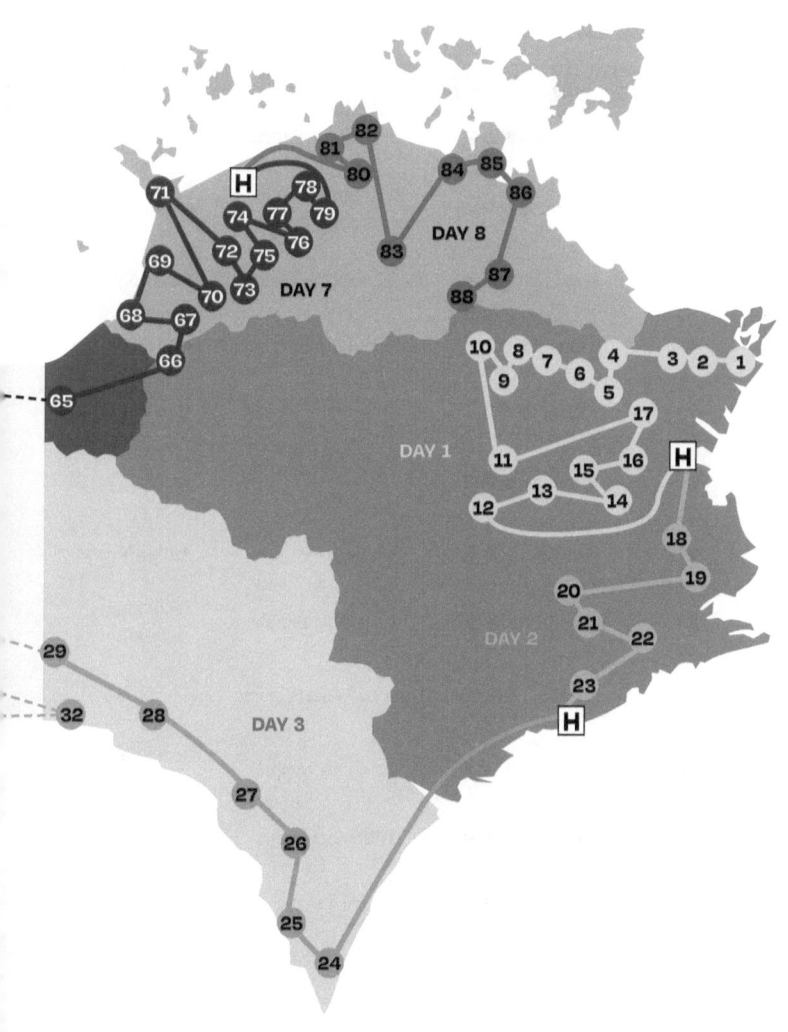

OUR ITINERARY

DAY 1

Tokushima Prefecture
Dojo of Spiritual Awakening, Temples 1 to 17

TEMPLE	NAME IN JAPANESE	NAME IN ENGLISH	MAIN IMAGE
1	Ryozenji (霊山寺)	Vulture Peak Temple	Shaka Nyorai
1.2 km (2 min)			
2	Gokurakuji (極楽寺)	Pure Land Temple or Paradise Temple	Amida Nyorai
2.6 km (5 min)			
3	Konsenji (金泉寺)	Golden Spring Temple	Shaka Nyorai
6.4 km (14 min)			
4	Dainichiji (大日寺)	Temple of the Great Sun	Dainichi Nyorai
1.7 km (6 min)			
5	Jizoji (地蔵寺)	Earthbearer's Temple	Shogun Jizo Bosatsu
5.2 km (10 min)			
6	Anrakuji (安楽寺)	Temple of Everlasting Joy	Yakushi Nyorai
1.2 km (4 min)			
7	Jurakuji (十楽寺)	Temple of Ten Joys	Amida Nyorai
3.8 km (5 min)			
8	Kumadaniji (熊谷寺)	Bear Valley Temple	Senju Kannon Bosatsu
2.6 km (6 min)			
9	Horinji (法輪寺)	Dharma Wheel Temple	Reclining Shaka Nyorai
4.5 km (12 min)			
10	Kirihataji (切幡寺)	Cut Cloth Temple	Senju Kannon Bosatsu
10.9 km (26 min)			
11	Fujiidera (藤井寺)	Wisteria Temple	Yakushi Nyorai
15.7km (30 min)			
*17	Idoji (井戸寺)	Well Temple	Yakushi Nyorai
3.7 km (10 min)			
*16	Kannonji (観音寺)	Avalokitesvara Temple	Senju Kannon Bosatsu
2.2 km (6 min)			
*15	Kokubunji (國分寺)	Official State Temple of Tokushima	Yakushi Nyorai
0.9 km (3 min)			

*14	Jorakuji (常楽寺)	Temple of Everlasting Peace	Miroku Bosatsu
2.8 km (7 min)			
*13	Dainichiji (大日寺)	Temple of the Great Sun	Juichimen Kannon Bosatsu
26.4 km (40 min)			
*12	Shosanji or Shozanji (焼山寺)	Burning Mountain Temple	Kokuzo Bosatsu
34 km (59 min)			
Accommodation: A hotel in Tokushima City in Tokushima Prefecture			

DAY 2

Tokushima Prefecture
Dojo of Spiritual Awakening, Temples 18 to 23

TEMPLE	NAME IN JAPANESE	NAME IN ENGLISH	MAIN IMAGE
Distance from our accommodation the previous night: 11 km (25 min)			
18	Onzanji (恩山寺)	Temple of Gratitude Mountain	Yakushi Nyorai
4.5 km (8 min)			
19	Tatsueji (立江寺)	Temple of Arising Bay	Enmei (Enmyo) Jizo Bosatsu
16.5 km (27 min)			
20	Kakurinji (鶴林寺)	Crane Forest Temple	Jizo Bosatsu
11.3 km (20 min to the ropeway platform)			
21	Tairyuji (太竜寺)	Great Dragon Temple	Kokuzo Bosatsu
13.4 km (17 min from the ropeway platform)			
22	Byodoji (平等寺)	Temple of Equality	Yakushi Nyorai
18.8 km (21 min)			
23	Yakuoji (薬王寺)	Medicine King Temple	Yakushi Nyorai
0.2 km (1 min)			
Accommodation: A hotel just in front of the JR Hiwasa Station in Tokushima Prefecture, literally a minute from Temple 23			

DAY 3
Kochi Prefecture
Dojo of Ascetic Training, Temples 24 to 34

TEMPLE	NAME IN JAPANESE	NAME IN ENGLISH	MAIN IMAGE
Distance from our accommodation the previous night: 77.1 km (80 min)			
24	Hotsumisakiji (最御崎寺)	Cape Temple	Kokuzo Bosatsu
6.5 km (12 min)			
25	Shinshoji (津照寺)	Temple of the Illuminating Seaport	Kajitori Enmei Jizo Bosatsu
5.2 km (11 min)			
26	Kongochoji (金剛頂寺)	Vajra Peak Temple	Yakushi Nyorai
34.2 km (52 min)			
27	Konomineji (神峰寺)	God's Summit Temple	Juichimen Kannon Bosatsu
37.4 km (58 min)			
28	Dainichiji (大日寺)	Great Sun Temple	Dainichi Nyorai
11.3 km (20 min)			
29	Kokubunji (国分寺)	Official State Temple of Kochi Prefecture	Senju Kannon Bosatsu
7.7 km (14 min)			
30	Zenrakuji or Anrakuji (善楽寺)	Temple of True Joy or Temple of Everlasting Joy	Amida Nyorai
8.6 km (19 min)			
31	Chikurinji (竹林寺)	Bamboo Forest Temple	Monju Bosatsu
6.9 km (17 min)			
32	Zenjibuji (禅師峰寺)	Temple of Ch'an Master's Peak	Juichimen Kannon Bosatsu
10.7 km (19 min)			
33	Sekkeiji (雪蹊寺)	Snowy Cliff Temple	Yakushi Nyorai
7.3 km (12 min)			
34	Tanemaji (種間寺)	Sowing Seeds Temple	Yakushi Nyorai
12.8 km (24 min)			
Accommodation: A hotel near Harimaya Bridge in Kochi City, Kochi Prefecture			

DAY 4

Kochi Prefecture
Dojo of Ascetic Training, Temples 35 to 39

TEMPLE	NAME IN JAPANESE	NAME IN ENGLISH	MAIN IMAGE
Distance from our accommodation the previous night: 18.8 km (36 min)			
35	Kiyotakiji (清滝寺)	Clean Waterfall Temple	Yakushi Nyorai
13.9 km (24 min)			
36	Shoryuji (青龍寺)	Green Dragon Temple	Fudo Myoo
53.1 km (56 min)			
37	Iwamotoji (岩本寺)	Rocky Root Temple	Amida Nyorai Yakushi Nyorai Kannon Bosatsu Jizo Bosatsu Fudo Myoo
87.6 km (110 min)			
38	Kongofukuji (金剛福寺)	Temple of Everlasting Happiness	Senju Kannon Bosatsu
54.9 km (75 min)			
39	Enkoji (延光寺)	Emitting Light Temple	Yakushi Nyorai
28.5 km (40 min)			
Accommodation: A hotel near Temple 40, the first temple to be visited the following day			

DAY 5

Ehime Prefecture
Dojo of Enlightenment, Temples 40 to 51

TEMPLE	NAME IN JAPANESE	NAME IN ENGLISH	MAIN IMAGE
Distance from our accommodation the previous night: 1.2 km (3 min)			
40	Kanjizaiji (観自在寺)	Temple of Kannon	Yakushi Nyorai
50.7 km (58 min)			
41	Ryukoji (龍光寺)	Dragon's Ray Temple	Juichimen Kannon Bosatsu
4 km (6 min)			
42	Butsumokuji (佛木寺)	Temple of Buddha's Tree	Dainichi Nyorai
17.6 km (21 min)			
43	Meisekiji (明石寺)	Brilliant Stone Temple	Senju Kannon Bosatsu
76.2 km (83 min)			
44	Daihoji or Taihoji (大寶寺)	Great Treasure Temple	Juichimen Kannon Bosatsu
12.3 km (22 min)			
45	Iwayaji (岩屋寺)	Rock Cave Temple	Fudo Myoo
34.1 km (47 min)			
46	Joruriji (浄瑠璃寺)	Pure Emerald Temple	Yakushi Nyorai
1 km (5 min)			
47	Yasakaji (八坂寺)	Temple of Eight Slopes	Amida Nyorai
4.8 km (16 min)			
48	Sairinji (西林寺)	West Forest Temple	Juichimen Kannon Bosatsu
3.4 km (12 min)			
49	Jodoji (浄土寺)	Pure Land Temple	Shaka Nyorai
2.4 km (7 min)			
50	Hantaji (繁多寺)	Temple of Great Prosperity	Yakushi Nyorai
2.9 km (9 min)			
51	Ishiteji (石手寺)	Stone Hand Temple	Yakushi Nyorai
3.46 km (7 min)			
Accommodation: A hotel near Matsuyama Castle in Ehime Prefecture			

DAY 6

Ehime Prefecture
Dojo of Enlightenment, Temples 52 to 64

TEMPLE	NAME IN JAPANESE	NAME IN ENGLISH	MAIN IMAGE
Distance from our accommodation the previous night: 8 km (20 min)			
52	Taisanji or Taizanji (太山寺)	Big Mountain Temple	Juichimen Kannon Bosatsu
2.5 km (10 min)			
53	Enmyoji or Emmyoji (円明寺)	Temple of Circular Illumination	Amida Nyorai
36.6 km (54 min)			
54	Enmeiji or Emmeiji (延命寺)	Temple of Long Life	Fudo Myoo
4.3 km (14 min)			
55	Nankobo (南光坊)	Temple of Southern Lights	Daitsu Chisho Nyorai
3.4 km (9 min)			
56	Taisanji (泰山寺)	Peace Mountain Temple	Jizo Bosatsu
3.1 km (9 min)			
57	Eifukuji (栄福寺)	Temple of Good Luck	Amida Nyorai
5.2 km (15 min)			
58	Senyuji (仙遊寺)	Hermit in Seclusion Temple	Senju Kannon Bosatsu
7.9 km (18 min)			
59	Kokubunji (国分寺)	Official State Temple of Ehime Prefecture	Yakushi Nyorai
18.3 km (30 min)			
*61	Koonji (香園寺)	Incense Garden Temple	Dainichi Nyorai
1.5 km (5 min)			
62	Hojuji (宝寿寺)	Temple of Wealth and Happiness	Juichimen Kannon Bosatsu
1.3 km (3 min)			
63	Kichijoji (吉祥寺) (also read as Kisshoji)	Temple of Mahasri or Laksmi	Bishamonten
3.2 km (5 min)			
64	Maegamiji (前神寺)	Front God Temple	Amida Nyorai
14.6 km (24 min)			
*60	Yokomineji (横峰寺)	Side Summit or Peak Temple	Dainichi Nyorai
53.6 km (50 min)			
Accommodation: A hotel near Iyo Mishima Station			

DAY 7

Ehime Prefecture
Dojo of Enlightenmen, Temple 65

Kagawa Prefecture
Dojo of Nirvana, Temples 66 to 79

TEMPLE	NAME IN JAPANESE	NAME IN ENGLISH	MAIN IMAGE
Distance from our accommodation the previous night: 8.4 km (23 min)			
65	Sankakuji (三角寺)	Triangle Temple	Juichimen Kannon Bosatsu
29.3 km to the ropeway platform (37 min) plus 2.6 km on the ropeway (7 min)			
66	Unpenji (雲辺寺)	Hovering Clouds Temple	Senju Kannon Bosatsu
11.2 km (21 min) from Unpenji ropeway platform			
67	Daikoji (大興寺)	Temple of the Great Growth	Yakushi Nyorai
10.1 km (22 min)			
68	Jinnein (神恵院)	Temple of God's Grace	Amida Nyorai
0 km			
69	Kannonji (観音寺)	Temple of Kannon	Sho Kannon Bosatsu
5.3 km (11 min)			
70	Motoyamaji (本山寺)	Headquarters Temple	Bato Kannon Bosatsu
12.6 km (25 min)			
71	Iyadaniji (弥谷寺)	Eight Valley Temple	Senju Kannon Bosatsu
5.3 km (16 min)			
72	Mandaraji (曼荼羅寺)	Mandala Temple	Dainichi Nyorai
0.55 km (3 min)			
73	Shusshakaji (出釈迦寺)	Temple of Shaka Nyorai's Appearance	Shaka Nyorai
3.1 km (8 min)			
*75	Zentsuji (善通寺)	Right Path Temple	Yakushi Nyorai
1.8 km (5 min)			
*74	Koyamaji (甲山寺)	Armour Mountain Temple	Yakushi Nyorai
3.4 km (7 min)			
*76	Konzoji (金倉寺)	Golden Storehouse Temple	Yakushi Nyorai
4.3 km (9 min)			
77	Doryuji (道隆寺)	Temple of Arising Way	Yakushi Nyorai

7.3 km (19 min)			
78	Goshoji (郷照寺)	Temple of Illuminating Local Site	Amida Nyorai
6.9 km (16 min)			
79	Tennoji or Koshoin (天皇寺)	Emperor's Temple	Juichimen Kannon Bosatsu
19.5 km (25 min)			
Accommodation: A hotel in the centre of Zentsuji City			

DAY 8

Kagawa Prefecture
Dojo of Nirvana, Temples 80 to 88

TEMPLE	NAME IN JAPANESE	NAME IN ENGLISH	MAIN IMAGE
Distance from our accommodation the previous night: 23 km (26 min)			
80	Kokubunji (国分寺)	Official State Temple of Kagawa Prefecture	Juichimen–Senju Kannon Bosatsu
13.6 km (23 min)			
81	Shiromineji (白峯寺)	White Peak Temple	Senju Kannon Bosatsu
7.3 km (12 min)			
82	Negoroji (根香寺)	Fragrant Root Temple	Senju Kannon Bosatsu
18.8 km (33 min)			
83	Ichinomiyaji (一宮寺)	First Shrine Temple	Sho Kannon Bosatsu
16.5 km (38 min)			
84	Yashimaji (屋島寺)	Roof Island Temple	Juichimen–Senju Kannon Bosatsu
7.3km (23 min) + Yakuri cable car (4 min)			
85	Yakuriji (八栗寺)	Eight Chestnuts Temple	Sho Kannon Bosatsu
6.8 km from the cable-car station (13 min)			
86	Shidoji (志度寺)	Temple of Fulfilling One's Wish	Juichimen Kannon Bosatsu
7 km (14 min)			
87	Nagaoji (長尾寺)	Long Tail Temple	Sho Kannon Bosatsu
16.7 km (25 min)			
88	Okuboji (大窪寺)	Large Hollow Temple	Yakushi Nyorai
to the next temple: Temple 1 – Ryozenji: 40.1 km (53 min)			
to Takamatsu Airport 26.2 km (40 min)			

V

NOTES

ENDNOTES

THE PAUSE

1. Reader, *Making Pilgrimages*, 45.
2. See Kūkai, *Kūkai: Major Works*, trans. Yoshito S. Hakeda, 1–11. Hakeda's introductory chapter on the life, thought and works of Kukai provides an insightful account of the 'father of Japanese culture', one of the most respected and popular Buddhist masters of Japan.
3. Toshikazu Shinno, *Tabi no naka no shukyo* (Tokyo: NHK Books, 1980), *Nihon yugyo shukyoron* (Tokyo: Yoshikawa Kobunkan, 1991a) and *Set naru tabi* (Tokyo: Tokyodo, 1991b) as quoted in Reader, *Making Pilgrimages*, 9. Reader mentions that the Shikoku pilgrimage stands out as a highly notable and visually appealing journey in Japan, a country renowned for its elaborate pilgrimage tradition.

I: THE NUDGE

Stories and Surprises

1. There are various versions of this story in Kukai's life. I have drawn this account from Nicoloff, *Sacred Kōyasan*, 18. See also Tanabe, 'The Founding of Mount Koya and Kukai's Eternal Meditation', in *Religions of Japan in Practice*. In the section on 'A Record of the Practices and the Establishment of the Temple of the Diamond Peak' is an account of how, in early March 835 C.E., Kukai predicted his passing.
2. Shiba, *Kukai the Universal*, 7, explains that the legendary tales associated with Kukai were actually propagated by wandering monks called Koya *hijiri*, who travelled across Japan to raise funds for Koyasan. In 'The Founding of Mount Koya and Kukai's Eternal Meditation', Tanabe argues that, while Mount Koya could survive without its philosophical roots, the absence of its mythical stories would significantly diminish its appeal to the public.
3. See Reader, *Making Pilgrimages*, 22–23, for an explanation of the history behind the practice of *nokyo* – getting the temple seal (*shuin*) imprinted on the pilgrim's stamp book (*nokyocho*) – and how this has evolved over time. See also Reader, *Pilgrimage: A Very Short Introduction*, 92.

II: THE JOURNEY

DAY 1
Routes and Rituals

1. The link to Katsuji's YouTube videos of our Shikoku Pilgrimage is: *https://m.youtube.com/channel/ UCEcqcR0jFmRB_yQ2wxDuHHA/*.

2. See Pye, *Japanese Buddhist Pilgrimage*, 165–168. This section provides useful context and information on the less well-known Tokyo Ten Shrines Pilgrimage (Tokyo *jissha meguri*).

3. Ibid., 75–102. Chapter 3, 'The Shikoku Pilgrimage', is a good introduction to the Shikoku pilgrimage that includes its origins, its route, the four stages through the four ancient provinces of Shikoku, its 88 temples and principal images.

4. Statler, *Japanese Pilgrimage*, 26. Written in 1983 by Oliver Statler (1915–2002), an American author and Japanese arts expert, this beautiful and moving travel diary remains a staple reference for those interested in the Shikoku route. I would have liked to have read this book before my journey, but reading it after my pilgrimage has brought an even deeper appreciation for the experience.

5. See Kitagawa, *On Understanding Japanese Religion*, 182–202. This is an interesting read on 'Kukai the Master' juxtaposed with 'Kukai the Saviour', sifting through historical fact and the abounding legends on the paradigmatic figure that is Kukai.

6. For references to *osettai* in this chapter and in a later section, I consulted the following: Reader, *Making Pilgrimages*, 122–126, and the brochures *The Eighty-Eight Temples and Pilgrimage Route of Shikoku* and *A Basic Guide to the Shikoku Pilgrimage*.

DAY 2
Legends and Landscapes

1. For the details of Kukai's life, I have drawn from the following: Kūkai, *Kūkai: Major Works*, trans. Yoshito S. Hakeda; Kitagawa, *On Understanding Japanese Religion*; Nicoloff, *Sacred Kōyasan*; Shiba, *Kukai the Universal*; Tanabe, 'The Founding of Mount Koya and Kukai's Eternal Meditation', in *Religions of Japan in Practice*.

2. See Shiba, *Kukai the Universal*, 37, for the origin of the idea of Miroku Bosatsu as the future Buddha who will come down to save the world.

3. I want to pay tribute to the labour of love of my mother, Dr Gundena M. Asprer, DMD, LLB, in writing the book *Dental Jurisprudence and the Regulatory Code of Dental Practice in the Philippines* (Quezon City: Rex Printing Company, Inc.), copyright 1990, reprinted November 2003.

DAY 3
Myths and Mountains

1. See Shiba, *Kukai the Universal*, 41–52. This section on 'The Morning Star Flew Into His Mouth' is an account of how Kukai was initiated into the practice of the mantra invoking Kokuzo Bosatsu and how he subsequently attained enlightenment in the cave at Cape Muroto.

2. Turkington, 'Overview', Pilgrimage on Shikoku Island, *http://www.shikokuhenrotrail.com/*. One of the more robust and comprehensive online English resources on the Shikoku *henro* and its various aspects.

DAY 4
Sights and Sounds

1. Readicker-Henderson, *The Traveler's Guide to Japanese Pilgrimages*, 47.
2. See this interesting research by Elisabetta Porcu: 'Pop Religion in Japan: Buddhist Temples, Icons and Branding'. *Journal of Religion and Popular Culture* 26/2 (2014): 157–172, https://www.academia.edu/10811568/.
3. For a light and entertaining read on bells in Japan, see Alice Gordenker, 'Pocket Bells'. *The Japan Times*, 18 May 2008, https://www.japantimes.co.jp/news/2008/03/18/reference/pocket-bells/. Her mention of bell-related *giseigo* (onomatopoeia) inspired me to incorporate some of this in the text.

DAY 5
Presence and Purpose

1. O'Brien, Barbara. 'The Essence of the Heart Sutra'. Learn Religions. https://www.learnreligions.com/the-heart-sutra-450023.
2. Kūkai, *Kūkai: Major Works*, trans. Yoshito S. Hakeda, 265.
3. See Kūkai and Kakuban, *Shingon Texts*, trans. Rolf W. Giebel and Dale A. Todaro with Kūkai's 'The Meaning of Becoming a Buddha in This Very Body', 54–70.
4. Statler, *Japanese Pilgrimage*, 129–130.

DAY 6
Faith and Freedom

1. Reis-Habito, 'Maria-Kannon: Mary, Mother of God, in Buddhist Guise'.
2. Reis-Habito, 'The Bodhisattva Guanyin and the Virgin Mary'.
3. Pitre, *Jesus and the Jewish Roots of Mary*, 182.
4. See Burmeister and Monte, *Touch of Healing*, 18. The section on 'The Foundation Concepts' states that the unobstructed flow of life energy through the body ensures perfect harmony. The sources of disharmony are the five basic attitudes of worry, fear, anger, sadness and pretence, which stem from FEAR (False Evidence Appearing Real).

DAY 7
Rendezvous and Redemption

1. There are various accounts of the legend of Emon Saburo. The account from Statler, *Japanese Pilgrimage*, 169–172, is my key reference for this section.
2. Reader, *Making Pilgrimages*, 255–257.
3. Ibid.
4. There are various versions of this story in Kukai's life. I have drawn this account from Nicoloff, *Sacred Kōyasan*, 21.

III: THE RETURN HOME

Monks and Mysteries

1. This legend appears in a number of accounts. Colourful details can be read in Kūkai, *Kūkai: Major Works*, trans. Yoshito S. Hakeda, 48; Shiba, *Kukai the Universal*, 269–270; and Nicoloff, *Sacred Kōyasan*, 45–46.
2. There are various descriptions of *shojin ryori*. I have drawn this description from Nicoloff, *Sacred Kōyasan*, 6–7.
3. See Nicoloff, *Sacred Kōyasan*, 124–132, for an explanation of the Dual Mandala and how Koyasan was constructed to be a physical representation of this.
4. Dougill, *In Search of Japan's Hidden Christians*, 224.

SELECTED REFERENCES

Books

Burmeister, Alice and Monte, Tom. *Touch of Healing: Energizing Body, Mind, and Spirit with the Art of Jin Shin Jyutsu.* Bantam, 1997.

Cousineau, Phil. *The Art of Pilgrimage: the Seeker's Guide to Making Travel Sacred.* Berkeley, CA: Conari Press, 1998.

Davies, Roger J. *The Japanese Mind: Understanding Contemporary Japanese Culture.* Edited by Osamu Ikeno. Tokyo: Tuttle, 2002.

Dougill, John. *In Search of Japan's Hidden Christians: A Story of Suppression, Secrecy and Survival.* Tokyo: Tuttle Publishing, 2012.

Dunskus, Oliver. *88 Temples of Shikoku: A Guide for the Walking Pilgrim.* Archtop Publications: Books on Demand, 2021.

Kitagawa, Joseph Mitsuo. *On Understanding Japanese Religion.* Princeton, NJ: Princeton University Press, 1987. (Kindle edition)

Kūkai and Kakuban. *Shingon Texts.* Translated by Rolf W. Giebel and Dale A. Todaro. CA: Bukkyo Dendo Kyokai America, Inc., 2018.

Kūkai. *Kūkai: Major Works.* Translated by Yoshito S. Hakeda. New York: Columbia University Press, 1972.

Lander, John. *The Shikoku Pilgrimage: Japan's Sacred Trail.* Bangkok: River Books, 2021.

Matsushita, Naoyuki and Moreton, David. *Visiting the Sacred Sites of Kūkai: A Guidebook to the Shikoku Pilgrimage.* 2014. (Kindle edition)

Miyata, Taisen. *A Henro Pilgrimage Guide to the Eighty-Eight Temples of Shikoku Island, Japan.* Los Angeles, CA: Koyasan Buddhist Temple, 1996.

Miyazaki, Tateki and Matsushita, Naoyuki. *Shikoku Japan 88 Route Guide.* Translated by David C. Moreton. Tokyo: Buyodo, 2018.

Nicoloff, Philip L. *Sacred Kōyasan: A Pilgrimage to the Mountain Temple of Saint Kōbō Daishi and the Great Sun Buddha.* Albany: State University of New York Press, 2008.

Pitre, Brant. *Jesus and the Jewish Roots of Mary: Unveiling the Mother of the Messiah.* New York: Image, 2018.

Pye, Michael. *Japanese Buddhist Pilgrimage.* London: Equinox, 2015.

Reader, Ian. *Making Pilgrimages: Meaning and Practice in Shikoku.* Honolulu: University of Hawaii Press, 2005.

Reader, Ian. *Pilgrimage: A Very Short Introduction.* Oxford: Oxford University Press, 2015. (Kindle edition)

Readicker-Henderson, Ed. *The Traveler's Guide to Japanese Pilgrimages.* New York: Weatherhill, Inc., 1995.

Shiba, Ryōtarō and Takemoto, Akiko. *Kukai the Universal: Scenes from His Life*. Tokyo: ICG Myūzu shuppan, 2003.

Sibley, Robert C. *The Way of the 88 Temples: Journeys on the Shikoku Pilgrimage*. University of Virginia Press, 2019. (Kindle edition)

Statler, Oliver. *Japanese Pilgrimage*. London: Picador, 1984.

Tanabe, George J. Essay in *Religions of Japan in Practice*, edited by George J. Tanabe. Princeton, NJ: Princeton University Press, 2020. (Kindle edition)

Periodicals

Proffitt, Aaron P. 'Who Was Kobo Daishi?', *Tricycle: The Buddhist Review*, 2018. *https://tricycle.org/magazine/who-was-kobo-daishi/*.

Reis-Habito, Maria. 'The Bodhisattva Guanyin and the Virgin Mary', *Buddhist-Christian Studies* 13 (1993): 61–69. Available at: *https://doi.org/10.2307/1389874*.

Reis-Habito, Maria. 'Maria-Kannon: Mary, Mother of God, in Buddhist Guise', *Marian Studies* (1996): Vol. 47, Article 8. Available at: *https://ecommons.udayton.edu/marian_studies/vol47/iss1/8/*.

Waite, Eric James. 'Stories of sky and sea: Storying the generational divide at Cape Muroto'. Thesis, Iowa State University, 2016. *https://lib.dr.iastate.edu/etd/15832*.

Websites

Iyer, Pico. 'Why We Travel'. Pico Iyer Journeys. *https://picoiyerjourneys.com/*.

Schumacher, Mark. Gods of Japan, A-to-Z Photo Dictionary of Japanese Buddhist and Shinto deities. *http://www.onmarkproductions.com/html/buddhism.shtml*.

Shikoku 88 Temple Pilgrimage. *https://88shikokuhenro.jp/en/*.

Turkington, Dave. Pilgrimage on Shikoku Island. *http://www.shikokuhenrotrail.com/*.

Brochures

A Basic Guide to the Shikoku Pilgrimage. Shikoku, Japan: Shikoku Henro Japan Heritage Council, n.d.

The Eighty-Eight Temples and Pilgrimage Route of Shikoku. Shikoku, Japan: The Shikoku Henro World Heritage Inscription Council, 2017.

Shikoku Pilgrimage: Experience the 1200-Year History and Culture. Shikoku, Japan: Shikoku Transport & Tourism Bureau, 2017.

GLOSSARY

Amida Nyorai – the Buddha of Infinite Light, also the Buddha of Limitless Life

Bato Kannon Bosatsu – manifestation of Kannon with a horse's head

Bishamonten – the god of war and punisher of evil

bodhisattva – one who has achieved enlightenment but postpones Buddhahood until all of humanity can be saved, helping others to attain enlightenment and transcend the wheel of life

bosatsu – the Japanese term for *bodhisattva*; the second category in the Japanese Buddhist pantheon of deities

Dainichi Nyorai – the Great Buddha of Universal Illumination, also the Cosmic Buddha

daishido – temple hall dedicated to Kobo Daishi; also called Daishi Hall or Great Priest's Hall

Daitsu Chisho Nyorai – the Buddha of the Past, who appeared prior to the historical Buddha, Shaka Nyorai (Sakyamuni)

dogyo ninin – loosely translated as 'we two travelling together'

dojo – a place to learn the way

Fudo Myoo – the Immovable Radiant King

hakui – white jacket worn by pilgrims

henro – pilgrim or Shikoku pilgrimage, depending on context

henro korogashi – a particularly difficult part of the pilgrimage route

historical Buddha – the former Prince Siddhartha Gautama (563–483 B.C.E.), who attained enlightenment; known in Sanskrit as Sakyamuni and in Japan as Shaka Nyorai

hondo – main temple hall, which enshrines the principal image of veneration

Jizo Bosatsu – known as the protector of children, travellers and women in childbirth

Juichimen Kannon Bosatsu – manifestation of Kannon Bosatsu with 11 faces

kami – native Shinto gods: the spirits of nature

kanji – Chinese characters used in the Japanese writing system

Kannon Bosatsu – the Lord of Compassion, also Goddess of Mercy; represented in many different forms

Kobo Daishi – posthumous name given to the Buddhist monk Kukai; see also *Kukai*

Kokuzo Bosatsu – the Bodhisattva of Wisdom and Memory, also Bodhisattva of Empty Space

Kongo Rikishi – guardians at the entrance gate who protect the temple from demons and thieves

kongozue – staff or wooden stick used by pilgrims

Kukai – founder of Shingon Buddhism, the monastic city of Koyasan and the 88-Temple Pilgrimage of Shikoku; see also *Kobo Daishi*

Miroku Bosatsu – the Buddha of the Future

Monju Bosatsu – Bodhisattva of Beautiful Splendour

__mudra__ – symbolic hand gesture in Buddhist and Hindu statues

__myoo__ – wisdom kings; the third category of deities in the Japanese Buddhist pantheon

__namu Daishi henjo kongo__ – mantra translated as 'homage to Kobo Daishi'

__nansho__ – a place that is difficult to reach

__nokyocho__ – the pilgrim's stamp book with pages folded accordion-style

__nyorai__ – Japanese honorific for one who has attained enlightenment or Buddhahood; the top category in the Japanese Buddhist pantheon of deities

__osettai__ – the offering of a gift, alms or a favour to a pilgrim

__sekisho__ – a spiritual checkpoint

Senju Kannon Bosatsu – manifestation of Kannon with a thousand arms

Shaka Nyorai – the historical Buddha; Sakyamuni

Shingon sect of Esoteric Buddhism – Japanese school of Buddhism founded by Kobo Daishi that asserts that everyone is born with the inherent potential to realise Buddhahood and that this can be attained in one's present lifetime

Shinto – Japan's indigenous religion, central to which are the spirits of nature called *kami*

Sho Kannon Bosatsu – manifestation of Kannon with one face and two arms

Yakushi Nyorai – the Medicine Master Buddha

In Gratitude

The crafting of this book has not been a solitary journey but a harmonious collaboration. It's the beautiful symphony of many voices, insights and hands that have breathed life into these pages – a testament to the collective spirit behind every individual endeavour.

First and foremost, a deep bow of gratitude to my travel companions Mayumi and Katsuji Hasegawa, whose friendship I dearly treasure. Mayumi, your deep-rooted understanding of Japan's history, geography, language and culture became my compass, enabling me to tread the Shikoku pilgrimage with understanding, grace and reverence. Your meticulous research and guidance ensured this narrative reflected the authenticity, depth and nuance of this centuries-old tradition. Katsuji, our travels were enriched by your camaraderie, humour and excellent driving skills; a journey remembered as much for the joy of the excursion itself as for its destinations.

Brian Seth Hurst, your coaching was like a guiding star, illuminating the path and potential within me. Through our enlightening dialogues, you turned my gaze inward, transforming a pilgrimage adventure into a heartfelt odyssey. Fern Lecuna, you lent a touch of creativity to this venture, and your friendship brought much delight to our shared endeavour.

Fr David Ranson, your wisdom and encouragement gave wings to my aspirations, strengthening my resolve and urging me on. Vikas Malkani and Sally Forrest, your teachings offered a lens of wisdom through which I viewed my world and experiences anew.

Angge Goloy and Cynthia Martin, you sculpted and refined the initial versions of my manuscript. Lucy Ridout, your editorial finesse transformed words into magic, honing this narrative into its finest form.

A heartfelt nod to Shin Matsuguma and my cherished Japanese friends and colleagues. The richness of your culture and generosity has left an indelible mark on both my heart and this work.

Rosie Pearce and the dedicated team at Whitefox Publishing Limited, your commitment transformed dreams into tangible pages.

Lastly, my deep gratitude to my husband, Roberto. In every shadow of doubt, your unwavering faith in me was the light. And to our sons Paolo and John you are the heartbeat and inspiration of every tale I weave.

To everyone who touched this project, my heart overflows with boundless gratitude.

About the author

From humble beginnings in Baguio City in the Philippines, Yvonne Corpuz blazed a path that led to distinguished leadership roles in prestigious global financial companies. While balancing the cherished roles of wife and mother, her dynamic career spanned academia, government and the corporate sphere, with international experience in Hong Kong, Australia, Singapore and Japan.

After a fulfilling three decades in the corporate world, Yvonne embarked on a new chapter in her life, with *Shikoku* marking her debut as an author. Her diverse life experiences combine with a powerful exploration of wisdom and spiritual insight to enrich this first non-fiction work. Yvonne currently lives in Sydney, Australia, with her husband.

First published in Great Britain in 2024 by
Yvonne Corpuz, in partnership with whitefox publishing

www.wearewhitefox.com

Copyright © Yvonne Corpuz, 2024

ISBN 978-1-916797-07-9
Also available as an eBook
ISBN 978-1-916797-08-6

Yvonne Corpuz asserts the moral right to be identified as the author of this work.

All rights reserved. No part of this publication may be reproduced, stored in a retrieval system or transmitted in any form or by any means, electronic, mechanical, photocopying, recording or otherwise, without prior written permission of the author.

While every effort has been made to trace the owners of copyright material reproduced herein, the author would like to apologise for any omissions and will be pleased to incorporate missing acknowledgements in any future editions.

All photographs and illustrations in this book © Yvonne Corpuz, unless otherwise stated.

Design by maru studio G.K.
Cover illustrations by Mayumi Hasegawa. Front cover illustration based on an original photograph by Akihito Yamamato
Internal illustrations and calligraphy by Mayumi Hasegawa
Photography by Yvonne Corpuz (pp. 23, 117, 139, 183, 221, 279) and Akihito Yamamato (pp. 67, 141, 219, 255)
Project management by whitefox

www.ingramcontent.com/pod-product-compliance
Lightning Source LLC
Chambersburg PA
CBHW030107100526
44591CB00009B/314